QUILTING TRADITIONS:

PIECES FROM THE PAST

Patricia T. Herr

4880 Lower Valley Road, Atglen, PA 19310 USA

DEDICATION

To Gerald S. Lestz, a visionary who brought to the public the need to preserve Lancaster County quilting traditions, and who spearheaded the Heritage Center of Lancaster County's Quilt Harvest Project to identify and document regional quilts.

Frontispiece:
Map of Pennsylvania quilt, "Made and presented W C C by grandma Carpenter, aged 78," made for William Cullen Carpenter. One of two Pennsylvania Map quilts made for grandchildren of Uriah and Harriet Carpenter. Designed by Uriah Carpenter (1791-1876) and executed by Harriet Miller Carpenter (1797-1876), Warwick Township, 1906. Pieced cotton top with cotton outline stitch decoration, cotton batting, cotton back, 73" x 84.5". *Collection of Fay C. Garman.*

Copyright © 2000 by The Heritage Center of Lancaster County

Library of Congress Cataloging-in-Publication Data
Herr, Trish.
   Quilting traditions: pieces from / Trish Herr
     p. cm.
  ISBN: 0-7643-1121-2 (pbk.)
   1. Quilts--Pennsylvania--Lancaster County--Themes, motives. I title.
  NK9112.H47 2000
  746.46'09748--dc21   99-086483

All rights reserved. No part of this work may be reproduced or used in any form or by any means—graphic, electronic, or mechanical, including photocopying or information storage and retrieval systems—without written permission from the copyright holder.
"Schiffer," "Schiffer Publishing Ltd. & Design," and the "Design of pen and ink well" are registered trademarks of Schiffer Publishing Ltd.

Design by Blair Loughrey
Type set in Americana/Korinna/Zurich

ISBN: 0-7643-1121-2
Printed in China

Published by Schiffer Publishing Ltd.
4880 Lower Valley Road
Atglen, PA 19310
Phone: (610) 593-1777; Fax: (610) 593-2002
Please visit our web site catalog at
www.schifferbooks.com
or write for a free catalog.
This book may be purchased from the publisher.
Please include $3.95 for shipping.

In Europe, Schiffer books are distributed by
Bushwood Books
6 Marksbury Ave.
Kew Gardens
Surrey TW9 4JF England
Phone: 44 (0)208 392-8585; Fax: 44 (0)208 392-9876
E-mail: Bushwd@aol.com
Free postage in the UK. Europe: Air mail at cost.
Please try your bookstore first.

We are interested in hearing from authors with book ideas on related subjects.

CONTENTS

746.46
HER

29.95 (17.97) Friends

4/02

ACKNOWLEDGMENTS

How does one select a few quilts to represent the thousands of wonderful bed coverings made in Lancaster County, Pennsylvania, over a period of almost 150 years? It can't be done! Other books must be written by people who wish to tell another story. But this story is the one that the quilts selected for this book have to tell us.

It would be impossible to fairly represent all the quilts and other objects identified and documented during the Quilt Harvest project (figures Ack-1 through 6) carried out by the Heritage Center of Lancaster County in 1988 and 1989. Even that sampling is not a true representation of the whole story of Lancaster County quiltmaking. The author has chosen a variety of objects from Quilt Harvest data, private collections, and other sources to hint at the diversity of the craft. Materials also have been gathered to help the reader understand the family and social context from which these quilts come. Certain patterns of quilts have been selected and grouped together to compare similar examples, noting how makers of various backgrounds and locations within the county chose fabrics and manipulated colors.

Ack-2
Quilt Harvest volunteer examining a quilt and gathering data for documentation in Ephrata, June 1989. *Image courtesy of the Heritage Center of Lancaster County.*

Ack-1
Quilt Harvest volunteers at various stages of examining and discussing quilts with owners at quilt documentation session held in Lancaster, December 1988. *Image courtesy of the Heritage Center of Lancaster County.*

If not for the Quilt Harvest documentation project, organized by the Heritage Center Museum, this book would not exist. If not for the dedicated, hard-working staff, consultants, and volunteers, the Quilt Harvest photographs, hand-recorded details, and computer database would not exist. It's not a simple matter to name all those involved, but to each person and organization that took part in the two-year process, the author and the Heritage Center Museum wish to express their sincere thanks.

During 1988 and 1989, the Quilt Harvest Steering Committee—Ellen Endslow, Evelyn Gleason, Linda Jermyn, Patricia J. Keller, Barbara Lenox,

Linda Jones McKee, Phyllis Thompson, and the author—organized and directed the almost impossible task of surveying and documenting quilts made in Lancaster County prior to 1945. To achieve this goal, documentation days were held in ten locations throughout the county within that two-year period. A further refining and gathering of information continues to the present day. The Steering Committee was assisted, at various times throughout the project, by Heritage Center Museum staff members: Associate Curators/Registrars Carol Kearney and Susan Messimer, Administrative Assistant/Public Relations Officer Diane E. Moore, Exhibit Preparator Lewis Bechtold, and Office Manager Frank Houseman. All of this activity was under the guidance of Director Patricia J. Keller, whose fine investigatory talents touched every facet of the Quilt Harvest study.

Two community organizations, the Red Rose Chapter of the Embroiderers' Guild of America and the Red Rose Quilters'. Guild of Lancaster County, mobilized their members to assist in the ten documentation days held at sites (figure Ack-6) throughout the county.

Members of these organizations and others who tirelessly volunteered their services are Irene E. Anderson, Luan Ashby, Georgia Behuniak, Jane Bibleheimer, Brenda Book, Anne W. Booske, Donna Bowersox, Mr. and Mrs. Brenick, Loretta Breniser, Lynn Brocklebank, Grace Brubaker, Kathleen Bucher, Mr. and Mrs. Colvin, Warren Conner, Jean Cook, Ridgely Cropf, Paul E. Danforth, Gail Dawson-White, Frances Deen, Maryann Dochter, Catherine A. Dux, Bill and Dorothy Edwards, Ruth Eshelman, Effie Eshelman, Deborah Federhen, Sandra Fulton-Day, Bill Day, Holly Girard, Naomi R. Glessner, Pat Grimes, Betty Guise, Ellen F. Hall, Janet Herman, Arlene H. Hess, Dina Hink, Marcia H. Hirneisen, Suzanne Hoffman, Jean Hoover, Robert and Alice Hostetter, Alex and Roland Jermyn, Judy Mark Knepp, Bonnie Knutsen, Peggy Krawizcki, Eugene and Dorothy Kreider, Linda Leayman, Bjorg Little, Jane Logdon, Julia Longenecker, Donna Lucidi, A. J. Many, Helen Mason, Rachel Monfredo, Arlene Mooney, Rondi Morris, Terry Nachwostach, Felice and Irene Nappi, Myrna Oak, Ann Parke, Tanna Parrett, Dee Perry, Donna L. Reinhart, Doris Reixinger, Kathlyn Reynolds, Nancy Riegel, Joanne B. Robertson, Ginnie Ruckert, Carol Slaymaker, Beverly A. Smith, Fred and Mary Spracher, Clayton and Marion Stehman, Shirley Stine, Grace Stirba, Patti Stone, Hilda Stork, Kathy Summers, Irene Svotelis, Alice Sylves, Charles and Virginia D. Thierfelder, Mary Alice Thompson, Donna Walter, Thelma Weaver, Charles and Betsy Weidler, Gloria White, Betty Wintersteen, Jane R. Young, Tom Young, and Robert and Pat J. Ziegler.

Recognition and appreciation are given to the several local banks that underwrote expenses of the on-site documentation. They are Bank of Lancaster County, Commonwealth National Bank (now Mellon Bank, NA), Fulton Bank, and Penn Savings Bank (now Sovereign Bank).

Consultants who shared their expertise with the Quilt Harvest project and this book include Barbara A. Brackman, Barbara G. Carson, Ph.D., Bernard L. Herman, Ph.D., Cathy A. Krall, Jeannette Lasansky, Rebecca J. Siders, Ph.D., Louise Stevenson, Ph.D. , Laura Thatcher Ulrich, Ph.D., Thomas Winpenny, Ph.D., and Shelly Zegart.

Ack-3
Quilt owners receiving conservation advice on storage of quilts from conservation staff and students from Winterthur Museum at Quilt Harvest site in Lititz, November 1988. *Image courtesy of the Heritage Center of Lancaster County.*

Ack-4
Quilt owners having a discussion with documenter at Quilt Harvest being held at Lititz. *Image courtesy of the Heritage Center of Lancaster County.*

Ack-5
Photography station at Quilt Harvest session held at Lancaster Mennonite High School, May 1989. Each quilt documented also received overall and detailed photography. *Image courtesy of the Heritage Center of Lancaster County.*

Ephrata

Elizabethtown

New Holland

Lancaster

Columbia

Susquehanna River

Quarryville

Ack-6
Map of Lancaster County pinpointing ten sites at which Quilt Harvest sessions were held during 1988-89. *Image courtesy of the Heritage Center of Lancaster County.*

Special thanks to Mary Jo Scott for sharing her time and research of the Carpenter family quilts and Clarke Hess, who is always a source of well-researched information. Others who have shared their expertise for the book are Kinsey Baker; Carolyn Ducey, Curator, International Quilt Study Center; Grace Miller Evans; Lucinda Hampton, Pennsylvania Dutch Convention & Visitors Bureau: Ed Hild of Olde Hope Antiques; Joanne Hess Siegrist; Elly Sienkiewicz; and John David Wissler. Most important is the constant love and support from my husband, Donald M. Herr.

Present Heritage Center Museum staff members Kim Fortney, Sandy Lane, and Wendell Zercher have been, as always, helpful and supportive. Special assistance has been given cheerfully and expertly by Nicole Bangert, Intern. All the staff activity has been accomplished under the watchful eye of Peter Seibert, our Executive Director, whose encouragement and leadership have never let us falter. Phyllis Thompson, Board of Trustees Member, has been with the project from its inception and has always given support when needed. Expert editing by C. Eugene Moore, President of the Heritage Center of Lancaster County, made this book more readable.

Above all, we thank the quilt owners who shared, and continue to share through the information in this book, their treasured heirlooms. We especially appreciate the help of those owners whose cherished objects appear in photographs within the covers of this book. They are Marianna N. Akerman, Geraldine Funk Alvarez, Mary Ellen Bachman, Keith Baum, Louis and Erla Mae Bowman, Anna Grace Brandt, Dorothy K. Habecker Brubaker, John H. Brubaker III, Marian Brubaker, Ruth S. Bryson, Sara Shaffer Bush, Roy H. Bushong, Sarah and Miles (Chip) Carpenter, Anna Mary Charles, Peace United Church of Christ, Covenant United Methodist Church, First Presbyterian Church of Lancaster, Pennsylvania, Long Memorial United Methodist Church, Alma F. Clendenin, David S. and Susan M. Cunningham, Mr. and Mrs. Lester Davidson, Betty Jean Herr Denver, John H. and Alice Ann Dinger, Roselyn C. Dommell, John W. Doughten, Sr., Barbara O. Eberly, Arlene M. Eby, Stella O. Esbenshade, Effie Eshelman, Linda S. Fahnestock, Harriett Carpenter Faison, Anna Mary Miller and Diane Fisher, Janet A. Fisher, Fay C. Garman, Isaac W. Gehman, Dorothy A. Groff, Erma Lois Herr, Arlene H. Hess, Clarke E. Hess, Dorothy Jean Hess, Ruth N. Hess, Raymond E. Holland Collection, the Hoover Family, Katherine Huddle, Robert L. Janney, Mabel B. Joseph, Stephanie Young Kaufhold, Patricia J. Keller, G.R. Klinefelter, Ron and Marilyn Kowaleski, Dr. and Mrs. Paul D. Kutish, Jay and Susen Leary, Marshall K. Long, Mitchell K. Long, Rebecca Hersh Longenecker, Herma R. Losensky, Minnie B. Metzler, Esther Hess Miller, Janet Sharon Young Miller, Virginia B. Mullin, Susan Patton Munn, Ruth A. Myer, Susan Patton Munn, Sheryl Quickel , Shirley H. Ranck, Shirley Redcay, Carroll M. Rottmund, Mr. and Mrs. John Salzmann, Nancy Scheid, Mary Jo Scott, Kathryn M. Shertzer, Evelyn L. Sinner, Gloria S. Smith, Roy and Lorraine Smoker, Lancaster Mennonite Historical Society, Edward S. Tochterman, Jr., Jim and Nan Tshudy, Alice Jane Herr Young Walter, Cynthia Welsch, John M. Whittock, Jr., Vivian R. Young, and Alice Zimmerman Anderman and Nancy S. Zimmerman.

—Patricia T. Herr

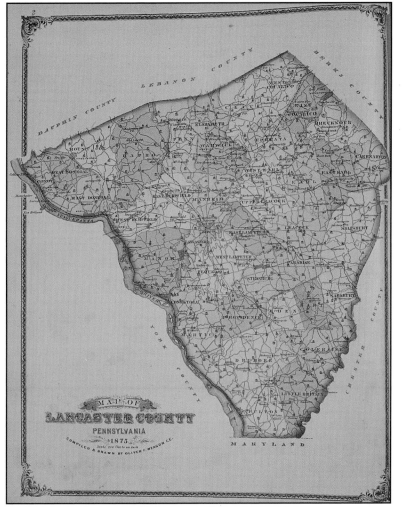

INTRODUCTION

Quilts made in Lancaster County reflect the diversity of cultures and comfortable lifestyles of early settlers in the region known, because of its verdant beauty and highly productive agricultural acreage, as the Garden Spot of Pennsylvania.[1] The flowering of distinctive styles in Lancaster County has resulted in a body of bed coverings recognized and prized throughout the world by museums, collectors, and art historians.

First carved out of Chester County in the southeastern corner of "Penn's Woods" (Pennsylvania) in 1729, Lancaster County (fig. 1) was reduced to its present boundaries in 1820. Because of its fortunate location, it became home to a diverse population of successful farmers and artisans. In this gently rolling land, with its productive limestone soil nestled between the Susquehanna and Delaware River valleys, close to the urban Philadelphia market, families flourished and set down deep roots. Bordered on the east by the predominantly English-speaking population of Chester County, on the north by the Germanic areas of Berks and Lebanon Counties, and on the south by the state of Maryland, Lancaster County became home to a richly diversified population.

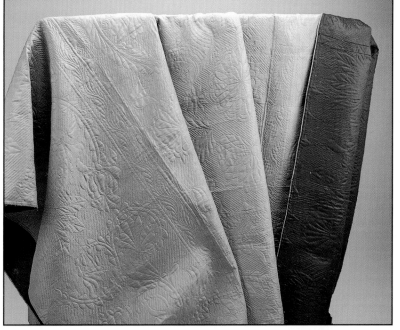

Above:
Fig. 1
Map of Lancaster County, Pennsylvania, 1875, compiled and drawn by Oliver F. Weagon, C.E., *New Historical Atlas of Lancaster County, Pennsylvania* (Philadelphia: Everts and Stewart, 1875), p. 2. *Private collection.*

Right:
Fig. 2
Whole-Cloth silk quilt with history of ownership in the Emlen family, early Quaker settlers in the Philadelphia area. Wool batting is consistent with English-style quiltmaking done in the 1700s. Maker unknown, England or Philadelphia area, mid-1700s. Silk top, wool batting, wool back, 103" x 99". *Private collection.*

Fig. 3
Double weave handwoven coverlet, initialed and dated " $\begin{smallmatrix} S \\ I \ E \end{smallmatrix}$ 1799," maker unknown, southern Lancaster County, 1799. Wool and cotton warp, wool and cotton weft, center seam, 82" x 78". *Private collection.*

The textiles in the book include examples made by at least three distinctive groups. The Pennsylvania Germans, the largest segment, dominate the selection. In the context of the book the Pennsylvania Germans include the obvious Anabaptist sects—such groups as the Mennonites, Church of the Brethren members, and Amish, all of whom believe in adult baptism. A variety of other Pennsylvania Germans including the Lutherans, Moravians, Reformed Church members, and German Catholics are included in this group of German-speaking people who emigrated to Pennsylvania in the 1700s and early 1800s. Small but significant bodies of quilts represented here were produced by the second group, the Scots-Irish Presbyterians, who settled in the southern and northwestern areas of the County, and by the third, the English Quakers, who populated the southeastern borders adjacent to Chester County and the State of Maryland.

These groups were drawn here because of the excellent farming conditions: moderate climate, highly productive soil, good water supply, and easy access to major population centers and markets. Because of their relative affluence and the availability of land, extended families flourished and strong community ties developed.

Within this context, the possession of a large quantity of material goods became the norm and a sign of status. Textiles, in all these cultural groups, made up a significant portion of valued household furnishings, as reflected in inventories and surviving family belongings. Those manufactured within the home, quilts in particular, became important objects that often reaffirmed

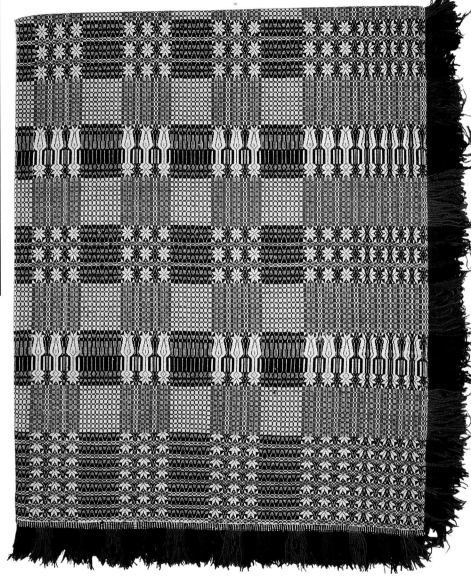

Fig. 4
Tulip-patterned multiple-shaft handwoven coverlet represents a complex weave structure, allowing for the use of figural motifs without the aid of advanced technology such as the Jacquard loom attachment. This highly sophisticated form of weaving was developed by the technically proficient southeastern Pennsylvania German weavers. Unknown male professional weaver, Lancaster County, c. 1840. Cotton warp, wool and cotton weft, center seam, 96" x 76". *Private collection.*

ties among family, friends, and community. Many of the quilts and related objects included in the book were made for specific persons or special situations. Quilts were commonly made for marriage, to mark the arrival of a new child, occasionally as a farewell to a minister leaving for mission work, or to raise money for a community organization.

Most of the earliest quilts found in the region were produced by the non-German population. Again, one may judge from inventories and surviving family artifacts from southeastern Pennsylvania, English families were making and using many more quilts in the late 1700s and early 1800s than were the Germanic households. One of the prototypes for these bedcovers is the whole cloth silk quilt (fig. 2) made and used by the first Quaker settlers in Pennsylvania. This particular quilt has a history of ownership in the Emlen family, early Quaker settlers in the Philadelphia area.

Lancaster County English families, the majority of whom resided in the southern part of the county near the Chester County border, also owned handwoven coverlets (fig. 3). The three-color doubleweave construction, often consisting of blue and red dyed wool and white cotton woven in a blocky plaid pattern, reflects the influence of Scottish weavers who also settled in the area.

Unlike the English, Pennsylvania Germans did not bring the quiltmaking tradition with them from Europe. Most households relied primarily on handwoven bed coverlets through the middle of the 1800s. Examples of

Fig. 5
Jacquard patterned handwoven coverlet made from multi-colored wools popular with Pennsylvania German consumers. Corner blocks located in the bottom corners of the coverlet give this information about the maker and consumer: "MADE BY/J.[JACOB]WITMER/MANOR/TOWNSHIP/FOR/ELIZABETH/FUNK/1844." Cotton warp, wool and cotton weft, center seam, 96" x 76". *Private collection.*

9

Fig. 6
Bed and bedding as they might have been used in a southeastern Pennsylvania German home in the middle 1800s. Handwoven multiple-shaft wool and cotton coverlet forms the top layer over feather tick covered with checked linen case. One linen sheet lies on top of two feather pillows and two feather bolsters covered with checked linen cases. All this lies atop a straw tick with plain linen cover that rests on a roped paint-decorated bed. The sleeper lies on the straw tick under the single sheet, feather tick, and coverlet. *Image courtesy of the Heritage Center of Lancaster County.*

coverlets commonly found in Pennsylvania German homes (figs. 4 and 5) differ markedly from the Scottish and English doubleweaves. A typical Germanic bed and bedstead of the mid-1800s (fig. 6) would be crowned with a coverlet woven by a local professional male weaver. Coverlet weavers, like many other skilled artisans, fled from Europe to Pennsylvania looking for peace and prosperity. They found ideal circumstances for settlement in southeastern Pennsylvania, with all the advantages of the area listed above and a population who were accustomed to and eager to purchase handwoven coverlets.

But by the middle of the 1800s Pennsylvania German women had learned the craft of quiltmaking from their English neighbors and had enthusiastically embraced the activity as a part of their culture. Similar piecing and appliqueing techniques were being used by both English- and

German-speaking women, and the confluence of these two cultural streams resulted in interesting and unexpected variations. Quilts from these diverse backgrounds can be differentiated by choice of color, fabric, and pattern. As time passed, techniques and patterns intermingled, producing startling combinations of color, design, and occasionally patterns that were unique to Lancaster County.

Fortunately, the geographic area remained productive and prosperous, preserving societal bonds. Family traditions remained, as did the material culture that accompanied their prosperity. By reaching out to the community, the Heritage Center Quilt Harvest project has been able to document many quilts and other textiles whose condition and historic background are intact. The following chapters are organized to allow these objects to tell their story of family, friends, and community.

Chapter One
THE QUILT MAKNG PROCESS

PIECING THE TOP

Most of the talented women whose quilts appear on these pages learned quiltmaking at home. Usually taught by her mother or another close relative, a child might begin working on a "starter patch" (fig. 7) by the age of seven or eight. Naomi Susan Ressler Howry (fig. 8) of Hessdale, Strasburg Township, completed her pieced square, based on a Nine Patch pattern, in 1870, at the age of eight. Although the family has no particular name for the piece, it has been used throughout the country under such names as Monkey Wrench, Churn Dash, Double T, Shoo Fly, and Hole in the Barn Door, to mention only a few.[2]

Quilting was a longstanding tradition in this Reformed Mennonite family, and Naomi learned quiltmaking from her mother, Mary Ann Miller Ressler. She used scraps and fabrics given to her by relatives for most of her quilts. After she married Edward Aaron Howry in 1881, she quilted frequently during the winter months by herself at home. There she had a quilting frame set up in a large bedroom.

Another member of the Howry family, Naomi's sister-in-law Mary Ann Howry (fig. 9), was also a quilter. Some of her tools (fig. 10) are still treasured by the family. Her brothers, Walter and Edward (who was Naomi's husband), walked to the Philadelphia Cenntenial Exhibition in 1876 from their home near the village of Willow Street, West Lampeter Township, and brought back the tape measure as a souvenir. No doubt this small gift was appreciated by Mary Ann.

Crippled by polio as a child, Mary Ann never married. She frequently traveled by horse and carriage to preaching assignments with her father, Christian Keeport Howry, a Reformed Mennonite minister and tailor. A talented needleworker, Mary Ann not only did the family sewing and fancy embroidery, but also worked along

Top center:
Fig.7
Starter patch, a form often made by young girls learning to quilt. Made at the age of nine in 1870 by Naomi Susan Ressler (1861-1942), Strasburg Township. Pieced cottons, 5.75" square. *Collection of Geraldine Funk Alvarez.*

Left:
Fig. 8
Naomi Susan Ressler (1861-1942), West Lampeter Township, maker of the starter patch (fig. 7), photograph taken before her marriage to Aaron Howry in 1881. *Image courtesy of Geraldine Funk Alvarez.*

Above:
Fig. 9
Tintype photograph, c. 1880, of Mary Ann Howry (1852-1939), sister-in-law of Naomi Ressler (fig. 8). Mary Ann, who suffered from polio, never married; she became a professional seamstress. *Image courtesy of Geraldine Funk Alvarez.*

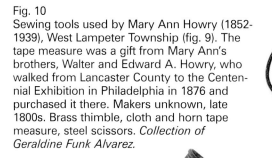

Fig. 10
Sewing tools used by Mary Ann Howry (1852-1939), West Lampeter Township (fig. 9). The tape measure was a gift from Mary Ann's brothers, Walter and Edward A. Howry, who walked from Lancaster County to the Centennial Exhibition in Philadelphia in 1876 and purchased it there. Makers unknown, late 1800s. Brass thimble, cloth and horn tape measure, steel scissors. *Collection of Geraldine Funk Alvarez.*

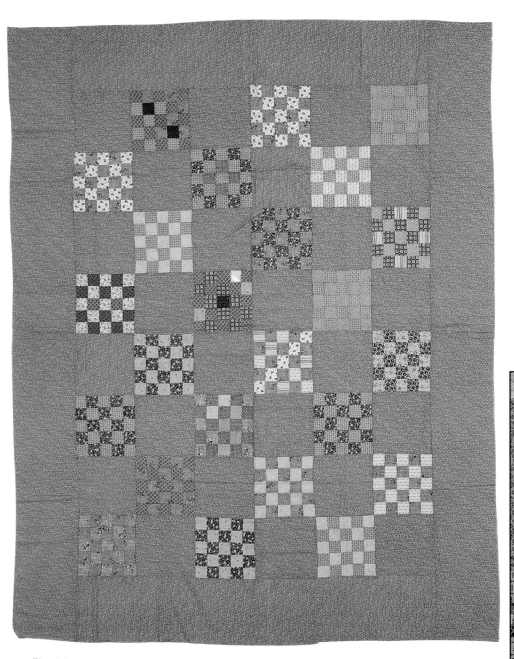

Fig. 11
Sixteen Patch unfinished quilt top pieced for family use by professional seamstress Mary Ann Howry (1852-1939), West Lampeter Township, c. 1920 (fig. 9). Pieced cottons, 71" x 58". *Collection of Geraldine Funk Alvarez.*

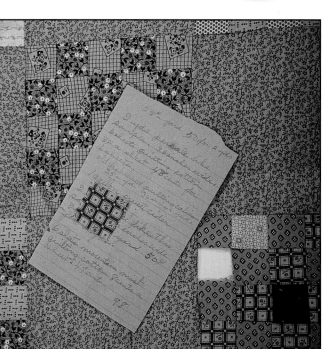

Fig. 12
Detail of Sixteen Patch quilt top (fig. 11), along with shopping list containing materials needed to complete quilt. Sample fabric patch cut from quilt and sent along with Mary Ann's niece to purchase two yards of matching percale. Assembled by Mary Ann Howry (1852-1939), West Lampeter Township, c. 1920. Pieced cottons and lined paper. *Collection of Geraldine Funk Alvarez.*

with her father in his tailoring business. Later in life she worked for Myers and Rafton, an exclusive tailoring firm in the city of Lancaster. She was also known in the community for her well-kept flower gardens. Mary Ann pieced, but never completed, a Sixteen Patch quilt top (fig. 11). Her shopping list, mentioning materials needed, and a sample of percale (which she actually cut from the quilt) are shown resting on her quilt top (fig. 12).

Paper and cardboard were the most common materials used to make templates for simple piecework such as Naomi's starter block. As a young woman in the 1920s, Martha Greider Herr (fig. 13) used paper templates as a guide for cutting out hexagonal shapes of fabric (fig. 14). She had previously made what she called a Flower Garden quilt and planned to make another. Martha's busy life which involved marriage, being a farm wife, baking for market, and raising a family, intervened in the process of making the quilt. She progressed no further on the project than her hexagonal patches, and these were stored away for more than 70 years.

Template quilt construction [3] is a method commonly used by English quiltmakers to join repetitive blocks. Partially completed quilt top sections (fig. 15) reveal how the method was carried out. Each six-sided patch was carefully folded around its own paper template. In this case the paper was recycled from what appear to be letters and account book papers from the late 1700s. The fabric was basted down around the paper and the edges finely whip stitched together on the back side. These examples probably date from the early 1800s and are often referred to as a Mosaic pattern. In the 1900s, when Martha Herr cut her hexagonal patches, the pattern was more commonly known as Grandmother's Flower Garden. Because template piecing is an English tradition, it is frequently seen in Quaker quilting. A number of the Quaker quilts pictured (figs. 71, 78, and 80) were pieced using the template method.

Fig. 13
Wedding photograph of Martha Greider Herr (1905-97), Strasburg Township, maker of Hexagonal patches and templates (fig. 14). Photograph taken in 1925 at the time of her marriage to Maurice G. Herr. *Private collection.*

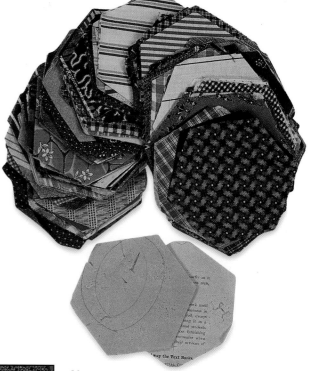

Above:
Fig. 14
Hexagonal patches and templates, cut out in the late 1920s and never made into a quilt by Martha Greider Herr (1905-97), Strasburg Township (fig. 13). Cotton and recycled paper, 5" square. *Private collection.*

Left:
Fig. 15
Hexagonal patches, pieced using English template construction method. Cloth has been folded, pressed and basted over recycled late 1700s account book and letter paper, then top-stitched together. Maker unknown, southeastern Pennsylvania, early 1800s. Cotton and laid paper, 9" square. *Private collection. Photograph by Donald M. Herr.*

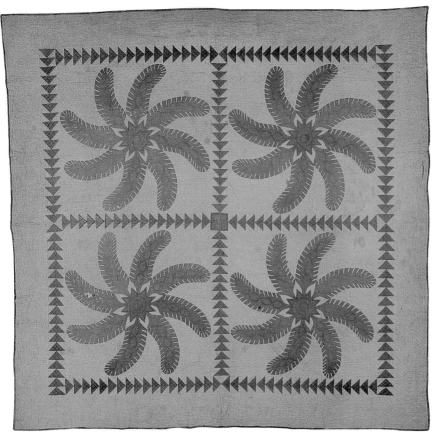

APPLIQUE WORK

More elaborate patterns were created with the applique method of quilt top construction. A template was placed on the fabric and outlined; then the fabric was cut, applied to the surface of the quilt, and stitched down. A signed and dated quilt (fig. 16) and applique pattern template used to produce it (fig. 17) are rare survivals that show the process. The central star area of the Princess Feather pattern quilt bears the signature and date "Mary Brubaker/1869" chain stitched on the surface. The accompanying pattern is also signed by the maker "Mary B. Brubaker Jan/1869." Although faded, the quilt was originally a deep brown and green on a yellow ground. Mary (fig. 18) made it in preparation for her marriage to Richard Henry Rickert on December 23, 1869. The Brubaker family belonged to the Reformed Church and lived in the Hammer Creek area of Elizabeth Township.

Once fabric choices for applique work were made and cut out, the quiltmaker's next step would be to arrange them as she wished on the ground fabric. A partially completed 1840s patch (fig. 19) illustrates this step. An unknown maker hand pieced a block design and began to embellish it by adding appliqued petals. The petals are held in place with large basting stitches and the applique process, with the needle still in place, is underway.

Above:
Fig. 16
Princess Feather quilt, signed and dated "Mary B. Brubaker/ 1869," just before her marriage to Richard Henry Rickert on December 23, 1869. Mary Brubaker (1844-1911), Elizabeth Township, 1869. Appliqued and pieced cotton top with chain stitching, cotton batting, cotton back, 85.5" x 88". *Heritage Center of Lancaster County through the generosity of Herma R. Losensky.*

Right:
Fig. 17
Feather applique template and detail of Princess Feather quilt (fig. 16), a rare survival of signed and dated quilt and template from which appliqued pattern was cut. Quilt signed and dated "Mary B. Brubaker/1869"; template signed and dated "Mary B. Brubaker 1 Jan/1869." Mary B. Brubaker (1844-1911), Elizabeth Township, 1869. Template: tan paper, 14.75" x 5"; quilt: appliqued and pieced top with chain stitching, cotton batting, cotton back, 85.5" x 88". *Heritage Center of Lancaster County through the generosity of Herma R. Losensky.*

Fig. 18
Mary B. Brubaker (1844-1911), maker of Princess Feather quilt (fig. 16). Daguerreotype taken in the 1860s before her marriage to Richard Henry Rickert on December 23, 1869. *Image courtesy of Herma R. Losensky.*

THE MIDDLE LAYER

The middle layer of a quilt could be a sheet, a light blanket, or even another quilt. The most common material found in Lancaster quilts is a thin layer of cotton batting. One of the companies making this material was, and still is, the Sterns & Foster Company, using the trademark Mountain Mist. Begun in Cincinnati in 1846, the company began offering free quilt patterns on their wrappers in the 1920s.[4] In the mid-1930s Barbara O. Eberly (fig. 20), a Mennonite quilter from Millway, tried out a pattern called Virginia Reel that she found on the Mountain Mist package. Using scraps salvaged from the local shirt factory, Barbara pieced the blocks according to directions on the wrapper just to experiment with the pattern. The preserved instructions and patches (Figs. 21 and 22) remain just as they were put away more than sixty years ago.

Fig. 19
Pieced and appliqued block, partially completed with needle and thread in place. Maker unknown, southeastern Pennsylvania, 1840s. cotton fabrics, 10.5" square. *Private collection.*

Fig. 20
Barbara O. Eberly (1919-), Warwick Township, photograph taken in late 1930s when she would have been working on her patches (fig. 22). *Image courtesy of Barbara O. Eberly.*

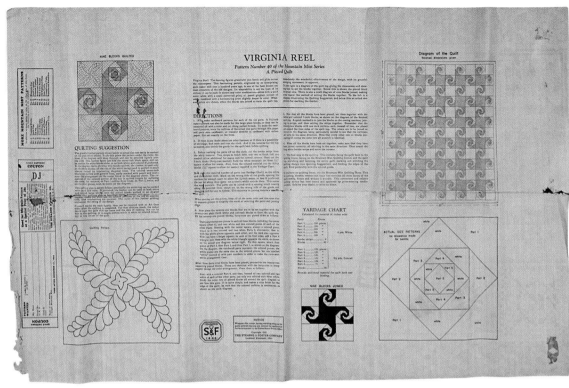

Left & above:
Fig. 21
Mountain Mist quilt batting packaging instructions for making Virginia Reel pattern. Virginia Reel patches pieced, using pattern insert, by Barbara O. Eberly (1919-), Warwick Township, 1930s (fig. 20). Paper, 33.25" x 21".
Collection of Barbara O. Eberly.

Right:
Fig. 22
Virginia Reel pattern patches, pieced from fabric remnants from shirting factory but never joined. Made by Barbara O. Eberly (1919-), Warwick Township, 1930s (fig. 20). Pieced cotton, 7.25" square.
Collection of Barbara O. Eberly.

QUILTING

With the top pieced and/or appliqued, and the filling and back in place, it was time to join the layers. A bedcovering could simply be tied or knotted as were many comforters. If quilting was used, it varied from simple geometric forms that followed the pattern in the top to intricate figural motifs designed and passed down through generations of quilters. Templates for quilting were frequently made of heavy paper or cardboard, but others made of tin, wood, leather, and various recycled materials also survive.

Jonathan Lowery made templates (fig. 24) for his wife Elizabeth Lenhart Lowery that he signed with his name and dated 1913 and 1924. He made a large variety, some for quilting and a few for applique work (fig. 117). The Lowerys (fig. 25) lived in the village of Lexington in Warwick Township, where he was a handyman. During the winter, when Jonathan was not as busy as at other times of the year, he used to enjoy making these patterns for Lizzie. In the early 1900s she had a stroke and was less able to get around but still continued to be an avid quilter.

Other less common materials were used to make quilting pattern templates, among them tin, wood, and leather (figs. 26, 27, and 28). Most likely these last three forms were also made by a husband for his wife.

Creating an intricately quilted white Whole-Cloth bedcovering (fig. 29) took a great deal of time, skill, and patience. The maker was Emma Bucher Brubaker Snyder (fig. 30), who lived near Lititz in Warwick Township. She made a similar

Fig. 23
Detail of Rising Sun quilt (fig. 141) with pieced strip back, characteristic most frequently seen in the northern part of Lancaster County, nearby Berks, and Lebanon Counties. Edge treatment of quilt shows how front was turned to back and stitched down. Made for Thomas Steffy by his mother Rose Wagner (Mrs. Uriah) Steffy (?-1926), Warwick Township, late 1890s. Pieced cotton top, cotton batting, and pieced cotton strip back, 83" square. *Collection of Stephanie Young Kaufhold.*

Quilt Backing

The quilt backing completed the three layers found in the traditional quilt. Fabrics used were plain, printed, or woven patterned materials. In approximately five percent of Lancaster quilts documented, the back consists of two distinct fabrics pieced in strips. Figure 23 shows a portion of a pieced striped quilt back. This construction is seen more frequently in the northern sections of the county bordering on Berks and Lebanon Counties. Rarely was a quilt reversible with a distinct pattern on each side. Other backing patterns, such as a Center Square with a border, are occasionally found.

Fig. 24
Templates for various quilting designs, inscribed in pen, with names Jonathan H. Lowry and Lowery, various dates. Made for Elizabeth Lenhart Lowery (1856-1943) by her husband Jonathan Lowery (1852-1926), Warwick Township, 1913-24 (fig. 25). Paper, cardboard, artist's board, oil cloth; varying sizes, 6.6" to 16". *Heritage Center of Lancaster County through the generosity of Herma R. Losensky.*

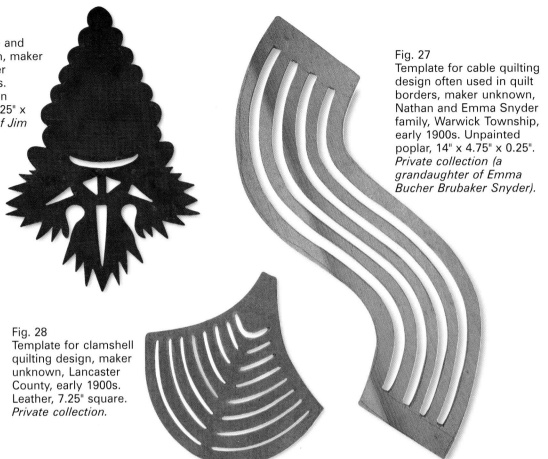

Fig. 26
Template for Grape and Leaf quilting design, maker unknown, Lancaster County, early 1900s. Recycled painted tin roofing material, 8.25" x 5.875". *Collection of Jim and Nan Tshudy.*

Fig. 27
Template for cable quilting design often used in quilt borders, maker unknown, Nathan and Emma Snyder family, Warwick Township, early 1900s. Unpainted poplar, 14" x 4.75" x 0.25". *Private collection (a grandaughter of Emma Bucher Brubaker Snyder).*

Fig. 28
Template for clamshell quilting design, maker unknown, Lancaster County, early 1900s. Leather, 7.25" square. *Private collection.*

Fig. 25
Jonathan (1852-1926) and Elizabeth (1856-1943) Lowery, photograph taken in early 1900s. Jonathan made quilting templates (fig. 24) for his wife Elizabeth. *Image courtesy of Herma R. Losensky.*

quilt for each of her four children and one for each of her eighteen grandchildren. The quilt pictured was made for granddaughter Erma Lois Hess. Her six grandsons each received a pieced quilt and her eleven granddaughters were given white bedcoverings similar to the one pictured. The twelfth granddaughter received a pieced quilt, like those made for the boys, because Emma's fine quilting skills had finally failed.

Emma's white whole-cloth piece was made of white sateen, the middle layer of cotton batting, and the back of less expensive white cotton fabric. The layers were held in place by well-executed quilting stitches all done by Emma's experienced hands. The penciled quilting lines are still visible on the front surface of the quilt.

As much quilting as Emma did, family tradition says that she had other women mark the quilting lines for her. One, a Mrs. Brubaker from neighboring East Petersburg, charged Emma $4 per quilt for her services. Emma Snyder was known for the fine quality of her white spreads, made mostly in the 1930s. She used only white cotton sateen for the tops rather than the unbleached muslin she employed for her pieced quilts. When not making quilts for her family, she did volunteer quilting with a group at the Lititz Mennonite Church. According to the family, she always had a quilting frame (fig. 31) set up in her sewing room.

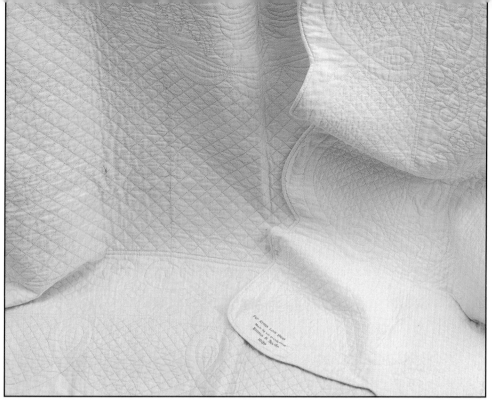

Fig. 30
Emma Bucher Brubaker Snyder (1876-1964), Warwick Township, who made white Whole-Cloth quilt (fig. 29). A grandmother of eighteen, she made eleven white Whole-Cloth quilts for granddaughters and eight pieced quilts for seven grandsons and her youngest granddaughter, c. 1946. *Image courtesy of a granddaughter of Emma Bucher Brubaker Snyder.*

Fig. 29
Detail of Whole-Cloth quilt with intricate quilting patterns as only surface decoration on bedcovering. Typed sewn-on inscription states, "For Erma Lois Hess/ Made by her grandmother/Emma B. Snyder/1939." Erma was born in 1929. Grandmother Snyder (fig. 30) made similar quilts for four children and ten other granddaughters. Emma Bucher Brubaker Snyder (1876-1964), Warwick Township, 1939. White cotton sateen top, cotton batting, cotton back, 79" x 78". *Private collection (a granddaughter of Emma Bucher Brubaker Snyder).*

Fig. 31
Four Mennonite women quilting at quilting frame set up in dining room of Enos and Annie Lefever's home in West Lampeter Township. Frame is similar to frame Emma Snyder had set up in her sewing room. Quilters are (left to right) Mary S. Lefever, Kate Bealler, Elizabeth Kreider Lefever, and Annie Stauffer Lefever. Photograph taken by Annie's son Harry S. Lefever, 1915. *Image courtesy of Lancaster Mennonite Historical Society, Joanne Hess Siegrist Collection, 2215 Millstream Road, Lancaster, Pennsylvania. 17602-1499.*

Of the Lancaster quilters surveyed, working in the late 1800s and early 1900s, 73 percent always did their own quilting and another 20 percent usually did. Over 87 percent of the makers studied owned a quilting frame and almost half of those frames were constantly or frequently in use. These frames were a familiar sight in Lancaster quilt maker's homes. Like Emma, almost 90 percent of these same quilters reported, at some time, quilting with a group.

EDGE FINISHING

When the fabric was taken off the quilting frame, its edges could be finished in a variety of ways. Sometimes the back was turned to the front and stitched down (fig. 32). The front could be turned to the back (fig. 23). The edges might also be butted together with no additional edging fabric (fig. 33). In the case of Emma Snyder's quilt (fig. 29) the edges were cut in a scalloped form, making it necessary to have a separate sewn-on cut fabric strip as edging. Almost all Lancaster Amish quilts are also finished with a separate piece of fabric, forming a border about one inch wide of a contrasting color (fig. 93). Quilts made in the early 1800s were frequently finished with a commercially woven cotton tape (fig. 47).

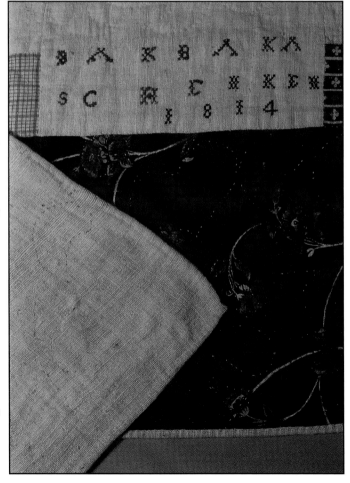

Fig. 32
Detail of Single Irish Chain quilt (fig. 49) showing cross stitched area along lower border, identifying owner or maker and date of quilt as "Barbara Schenken 1814." "En" is ending Pennsylvania Germans often use when writing a woman's name. Finishing the edges of this quilt required no separate fabric strip; the back fabric was turned to front and stitched down. Attributed to Barbara Schenk (dates unknown), Lancaster County, 1814. Pieced cotton top with cotton embroidery thread, cotton batting, cotton back, 91" square. *Private collection. Photograph by Donald M. Herr.*

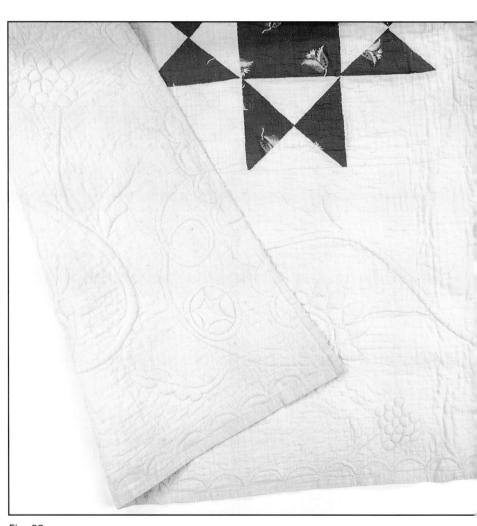

Fig. 33
Detail of Framed Center quilt (fig. 43) with butted edge; front and back surfaces have been folded in and stitched together. Maker/owner (Ann) Margaret Gundacker (1794-after 1883), Lancaster Borough, 1810. Pieced and appliqued top with stuffed work quilting, cotton batting, cotton back, 122" square. *Heritage Center of Lancaster County through the generosity of the James Hale Steinman Foundation.*

KIT QUILTS

Not all quilt makers designed their own work or chose fabrics, quilt, or quilting patterns to make a unique bed covering. Miriam Bertha Keener purchased her Bucilla Dogwood kit quilt (fig. 34) from a local department store in 1942. She was taught embroidery by her mother, Lydia Mae Barr Keener, a Presbyterian who joined the Mennonite church when she married Miriam's father, John Martin Keener. The quilt was purchased before Miriam's marriage to John Melvin Thomas, a pastor from Chester County, Pennsylvania. She kept it in this partially finished state in her hope chest. Materials for the quilt cost $3.98, and the embroidery floss added another $1.10 to the M. T. Garvin & Co. bill.

Had Miriam completed her project it would have looked like the quilt embroidered by Bertha Herr Metzler, a Mennonite woman living in East Lampeter Township (fig. 35). According to the family, she had help from a woman named Annie Good, who did the quilting. Bertha made it for the hope chest of her daughter, Arlene H. Hess in 1938. During the 1930s and 1940s scalloped edges were popular; they were seen in kit quilts and in quilts designed at home, such as Emma Snyder's white quilt (fig. 29).

Fig. 34
Partially completed Dogwood pattern Bucilla kit quilt and bill dated "12-2-1942," purchased at M.T. Garvin and Co. department store in Lancaster City for $3.95 plus $1.10 for embroidery floss. Assembled by Miriam Bertha Keener (1925-), Strasburg Township, whose photo appears with materials. Cotton material, paper, cotton embroidery floss, assorted sizes. *Heritage Center of Lancaster County through the generosity of Miriam Bertha Keener Thomas.*

Fig. 35
Dogwood quilt made from commercially produced Bucilla kit quilt similar to partially made kit (fig. 34). Kit quilts frequently have scalloped edges, as seen here. Embroidered by Bertha Herr (Mrs. Harvey) Metzler (1898-1972), East Lampeter Township, c. 1940. Appliqued cotton top with French knots and blanket stitch cotton floss decoration, cotton batting, cotton back, 88" x 76". *Collection of Arlene H. Hess.*

SIGNING AND DATING A QUILT

Fortunately for those who study and enjoy historic quilts, many quiltmakers signed their quilts in some manner. Some incorporated the maker's name and date and others identified the owner. Pennsylvania German quiltmakers commonly used counted cross stitching to sign or identify their handiwork and less frequently a chain or simple running stitch (figs. 32, 36, and 37). A small group of quiltmakers, located primarily in Warwick and Penn Townships in northern Lancaster County, marked their quilts with highly decorative large needlework lettering (fig. 38). Another method of marking was to use indelible ink, choosing a person with good penmanship to do the inscriptions (fig. 39). Some quilts were marked using a fabric stamping device (fig. 40 and 41).

It's hard to miss bold initials when they are used as part of an appliqued pattern on a pillowcase (fig. 42). Using quilting to identify the maker or owner is a more subtle method. Sarah Jane Mullen's quilting (fig. 119) continues to speak for many quiltmakers with her quilted message "When this you see Remember me When I am in Eternity. . . ."

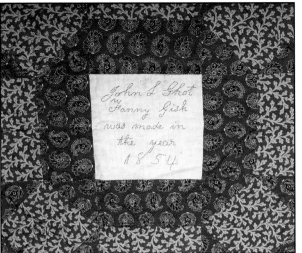

Fig. 37
Detail of Block Friendship quilt (fig. 63). Top left block identifies the quilt: "John L. Shot/Fanny Gish/was made in/the year/1854," probably made by friends of the couple. Fanny was an orphan and had no family to prepare for her marriage. Maker or makers unknown, northern Lancaster County, 1854. Pieced cotton top with red cotton running stitch, cotton batting, cotton back, 90" square. *Heritage Center of Lancaster County through the generosity of the James Hale Steinman Foundation.*

Fig. 38
Detail of Sawtooth Diamond (fig. 196), containing large embroidered initials placed prominently in center of quilt, a technique associated with northern Lancaster County (Warwick and Elizabeth Townships). Owner's initials "ARB" stand for Ada R. Brubaker (1882-?), attributed to her mother Lizzie Risser (Mrs. Peter Hess) Brubaker (1861-?), Warwick Township, c. 1900. Pieced cotton top with yellow cotton outline stitch, cotton batting, cotton back, 76" square. *Private collection.*

Fig. 36
Detail of Princess Feather quilt (fig. 144), chain stitched "Sue Hainly/1875" near corner on inner border of top surface, identifying quilt maker/owner as Susan Hainly (dates unknown), West Cocalico Township, 1875. Appliqued cotton top with red cotton chain stitching, cotton batting, cotton back, 90" square. *Collection of G. R. Klinefelter.*

Fig. 39
Detail of Papercut Friendship quilt top (fig. 73), many names written with ink in script on centers of appliqued blocks, attributed to Lydia A. Bradley (dates unknown), Drumore or Fulton Township, 1845-47. Appliqued and pieced cotton top, cotton batting, cotton back. 70" square. *Collection of Gloria S. Smith.*

Fig. 40
Detail of Papercut Friendship quilt (fig. 124), names applied in ink using fabric stamping kit similar to manufactured stamping set (fig. 41). Made by Amanda M. Hyman (dates unknown), East Cocalico Township, 1863. Appliqued cotton top, cotton batting, cotton back, 96" x 94". *Private collection.*

Fig. 41
Fabric stamping kit, "The Improved Linen Stamp," used by women to mark fabrics and possibly quilts with script alphabet and numerals; directions for use are on a label inside the lid. Possibly owned by Malinda Buch, whose name was set in stamp ready to mark fabric. Maker and location unknown, c. 1845. Steel, lead, wood, tin, in original cardboard box; box dimensions: 3.25" x 3.25" x 2.5". *Private collection.*

Fig. 42
Detail of appliqued pillowcase using owner's initials as part of decoration. Pillow case is one of set (fig. 203) that match similarly decorated quilt (fig. 204). "MG" represents the owner and possibly maker Mary Grumbine (dates unknown), New Holland, c. 1875. Appliqued cotton top, cotton batting, cotton back, 31" x 17.75". *Private collection.*

Chapter Two

EARLY QUILTS, 1800-20

Fig. 43
Framed Center quilt, earliest recorded dated Lancaster County quilt. Embellished with stuffed work, including stuffed work in central area containing initials and date "1810/MG," for Moravian maker/owner (Ann) Margaret Gundacker (1794-after 1883), Lancaster Borough, 1810. Pieced and appliqued top with stuffed work quilting. Cotton batting, cotton back, 122" square. *Heritage Center of Lancaster County through the generosity of Mrs. J. Nevin Schroeder, Jr.*

Fine quilts used by affluent Lancaster families in the early 1800s were usually quite large. The bedsteads and bedchambers of the period were imposing in size and design, so the bedcover for the master bed was often about 9 feet square. One such quilt (fig. 43) measures over 10 feet square and is the earliest known dated Lancaster County quilt. It is dated and initialed in the quilting "1810/M G." A detail (fig. 44) shows the stuffed work date and initials. According to family history, the quilt belonged to (Ann) Margaret Gundacker. It is appropriate that she, as the daughter of a prosperous Lancaster Moravian merchant, would have such an elegant bedcovering made in preparation for her marriage in 1816 to Robert Evans.

Margaret was well prepared for marriage in other ways, too. She and her sisters Elizabeth, Catherine, and Clementina attended the Lititz Moravian Girls' School, where they would have obtained a well-rounded education and exposure to the "Ornamental Branches" of the arts: music, painting, and fine needlework.[5] Moravians had high regard for education, and Moravian settlements in the New World had extensive resources to educate the children of the community in basic school studies and the fine arts. Records from 1805-06 from the Lititz school indicate that Margaret's father, Michael Gundacker, was billed for instruction she received in grammar, spelling, religion, history, music, and embroidery.[6] Margaret, who was born in 1794, was sixteen at the time the quilt was made. Her school needlework training would have enabled her, probably with the help of her mother, to execute this elegant spread.

Laid out in the classic Framed Center design first popular in the British Isles, Margaret's quilt illustrates the English influence on quilts made and used in affluent Pennsylvania German households. The design shows a masterful blending of pieced, appliqued, and stuffed work, enhanced by the elegant needlework of the Gundacker women.

In 1815, the year before her marriage, Margaret's father died, leaving his widow, Barbara Walter Gundacker, well enough situated that she was able to send Margaret's two younger sisters, Catherine and Clementina, to the Lititz Moravian Girls' School, too. While in attendance, one or both of the sisters executed the watercolor mourning picture (fig. 45), honoring Michael Gundacker. Margaret's af-

Fig. 44
Detail of Framed Center quilt (fig. 43). Central area stuffed work with "1810/MG," for (Ann) Margaret Gundacker (1794-after 1883), Lancaster Borough, 1810. Edge finishing done in plainest manner possible: turning cut edges in, butting together, and using no added fabric. Pieced and appliqued top with stuffed work quilting, Cotton batting, cotton back, 122" square. *Heritage Center of Lancaster County through the generosity of Mrs. J. Nevin Schroeder, Jr.*

Fig. 45
Watercolor Mourning Picture painted at Lititz Moravian Girls' School in memory of Michael Gundacker. His daughter, Margaret, maker of a Framed Center quilt (figs. 43 and 44), and at least three of her sisters attended the school. This painting illustrates the degree of sophistication in the arts taught at Moravian schools during early 1800s. Attributed to one or both of Margaret's youngest sisters, Catherine and Clementina, who were students after their father's death in 1815; Lititz Borough, 1821. Watercolor on paper; original reverse-painted glass; wood, gesso, and gilt frame; 27" x 26". *Private collection.*

Fig. 46
Framed Center Star quilt
containing a variety of
roller- and block-printed
and glazed cotton
fabrics, surrounded with
fine appliqued floral
baskets and devices,
multiple pieced and
appliqued borders, and
close-stipple quilting.
Attributed to a member
of the Gorrecht family,
Lancaster Borough,
early 1800s. Pieced and
appliqued cotton top,
cotton batting, and
cotton back, 101" x 110".
*Collection of Nancy
Scheid.*

fluent lifestyle would have continued with her marriage to Robert Evans, who was also a prosperous Lancaster City merchant.

The most elaborate of the group of early quilts (fig. 46) was crafted by a member of the Gorrecht family of Lancaster. Made in the early 1800s, it is a large spread—110 by 101 inches—suitable for covering the most important bed in an affluent home. The Framed Center design of the spread, like that of the Gundacker quilt, reflects the English influence on quilts made and used in affluent Pennsylvania German homes.

High-quality imported prints in a wide selection make up the central pieced star. Equally elegant block-printed floral design fabrics have been carefully selected, cut out, and appliqued to fill in between the points of the star and to build multiple outer borders. The feature that sets the quilt apart from the others described here is the close stippled quilting that covers the white ground. Not only is there an average of ten quilting stitches per inch but there are about ten rows of stitching per inch. A detail (fig. 47) shows the fine quilting and commercially woven tape binding frequently found on quilts made during this period.

Another Framed Center quilt dating from the early nineteenth century (fig. 48) was made from imported arborescent block-printed chintz material that was meticulously cut and appliqued on a white ground. Elegant quilting, filling the white areas, sets off the bird and floral design. Although the maker is not known, the quilt was found in the northeastern part of the county. Expensive chintz of this type was imported through the major eastern seaports in the late 1700s; it then found its way into many wealthy homes up and down the eastern seaboard of the United States.

A less sophisticated Pennsylvania German quilt can be seen in Figure 49. Composed of a simple Irish Chain design, it is set apart from the

ordinary by the cross-stitched annotation "Barbara/Schenken/1814," located just inside the dark print border (fig. 32). Barbara Schenk (with the Germanic feminine ending "en" attached to her name) was presumably the maker and/or owner.

Of much humbler origin than the previous quilts, this example is smaller in size; it consists of a coarser quality white cotton fabric and less quilting, and it contains no applique work. Nevertheless, it is made up of a choice variety of late 1700s and early 1800s imported and domestic dress fabrics. The quilting patterns within the white squares and border areas are also noteworthy as they represent a number of Pennsylvania German folk art motifs: eagles, pinwheels, hearts, and floral basket patterns.

Another well-documented Pennsylvania German quilt made in Lancaster County before 1820 (fig. 50) is also known. Although larger than the Schenk spread, it is of less sophisticated fabrics and design than any of the Framed Center bedcoverings. The choice of an orange print as a wide bright border imparts a definite Pennsylvania German flavor to the quilt. It appears to be an early signal of the common use of bright orange and yellow fabrics in later southeastern Pennsylvania quilts. One printed block in a corner of the quilt contains the barely legible poem, quilted in cursive letters, "Catharine/Myers the rose/is red the leaves/green here is my/name when I/am dead in/the year/1816." A close up view (fig. 51) reveals the small-scale block prints and the area that contains the signature. Except for the signature block, the overall quilting is coarsely done in a diamond or waffle pattern.

Catharine was the daughter of Henry and Barbara Brenner Myers, who were members of the Church of the Brethren. They lived on the family farm in East Donegal Township in northern Lancaster County. Catharine later married Peter Walter, who also was a farmer in the same neighborhood.[7]

Many affluent Pennsylvania German families, regardless of their religious affiliation, emulated the British styles when creating decorative household objects. In textile production affluent families frequently sent their young women to such schools as the Moravian Girls' School in Lititz or to day schools taught by schoolmistresses of English descent, where they were taught needlework in that tradition. The finest quilts, as seen here, are in the British Framed Center design and would complement the more refined Anglo-influenced furniture frequently owned by well-to-do German immigrant families.

The more typical Pennsylvania German families, the majority of the population of Lancaster County in the early part of the nineteenth century, would have been likely to hold to their Germanic roots when selecting bedcoverings. So it is understandable that handwoven coverlets were far more common in inventories and in numbers that still exist in family and museum collections today. Thus, one can appreciate that Lancaster quilts made in the first quarter of the nineteenth century are indeed rare survivals.

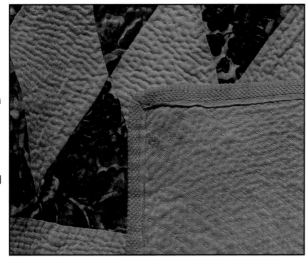

Fig. 47
Detail of Framed Center Star quilt (fig. 46), showing intricate applique fine-stipple quilting and commercially woven white cotton tape binding frequently used on quilts of this period. Attributed to a member of the Gorrecht family, Lancaster Borough, early 1800s. Pieced and appliqued cotton top, cotton batting, and cotton back, 101" x 110". *Collection of Nancy Scheid.*

Fig. 48
Framed Center quilt containing
arborescent block-printed cotton
chintz, heavily quilted by an
unknown maker, northeastern
Lancaster County, early 1800s.
Appliqued and pieced cotton
top, cotton batting, cotton back,
103" x 94.5". *Heritage Center of
Lancaster County through the
generosity of the James Hale
Steinman Foundation.*

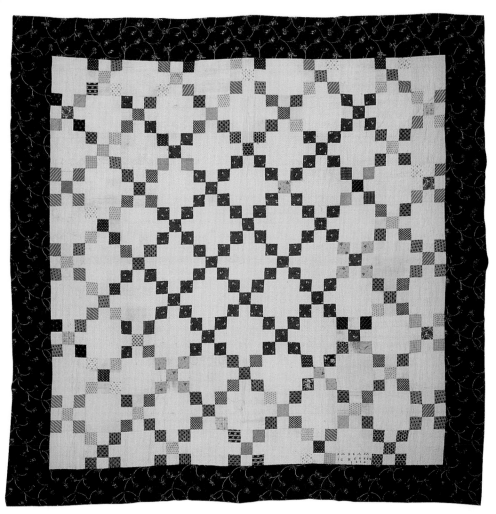

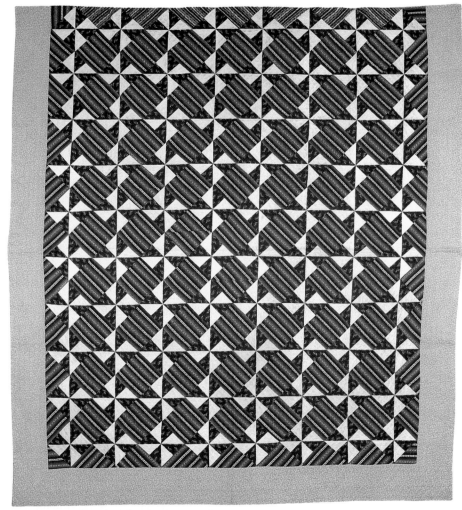

Above:
Fig. 49
Single Irish Chain quilt; cross stitched area along lower border (fig. 32) identifies possible owner/maker and date of quilt as "Barbara Schenken 1814." Fabrics appear to be variety of 1790-1814 dress fabrics, mostly imported. Quilting patterns in open white areas include eagles, pinwheels, hearts, and floral baskets. Attributed to Barbara Schenk, Lancaster County, 1814. Pieced cotton top with cotton embroidery thread, cotton batting, cotton back, 91" square. *Private collection.*

Above right:
Fig. 50
Block quilt of early 1800s dress fabrics; orange border print imparts a local flavor, forecasting a later affinity for bright orange and yellow by Pennsylvania German quilters. One corner block identifies the maker as Catherine Myers (dates unknown), East Donegal Township, 1816. Pieced cotton top, cotton batting, cotton back, 110" x 100". *Heritage Center of Lancaster County through the generosity of the James Hale Steinman Foundation.*

Fig. 51
Detail of Block quilt (fig. 50), showing corner block that contains the quilted information, "Catharine/Myers the rose/is red the leaves/green here is my/name when I/am dead in/the year/1816," Catharine Myers (dates unknown), East Donegal Township, 1816. Pieced cotton top, cotton batting, cotton back, 110" x 100". *Heritage Center of Lancaster County through the generosity of the James Hale Steinman Foundation.*

Chapter Three

RITES OF PASSAGE COMMEMORATED

Within the family, quilts have been used for generations to celebrate family rites of passage: birth, childhood, dowry (coming of age, marriage), and even death. They become a permanent part of family tradition, acting as a reminder of an event to be celebrated or mourned.

The purposes of these quilts, when they were made, were often to mark a specific event and to be used by the recipient. They have continued to be an integral part of many families' lives. They serve as commemorative objects, reminding family members of their ancestral roots. They strengthen family bonds, keeping the next generation in touch with past traditions. In many families the quilts give rise to another generation of quilting traditions. The descendants of Lizzie Kulp Buch (fig. 54), for example, continue to make quilts for each child's trousseau and as high school graduation gifts.

A quilt sometimes becomes even more of a personal reminder of an ancestor or close relative than a photograph is capable of being. Some families who are caretakers of these special family treasures gain satisfaction from sharing their treasures with the community and other historically minded persons. Quilts made with loving care often become intimate personal objects and continue to have subtle but strong effects on each new generation.

BIRTH

The making of a crib quilt is an obvious way to celebrate the birth of a child. Some new arrivals also received full-sized quilts like those made by Grandma Susanna Gehman (figs. 95 and 96). The most common practice for babies, however, was to make a small quilt.

Many of the more elaborate crib quilts appear never to have been used. This might suggest their commemorative nature as presentation pieces. The plainer variety, being more heavily used, would not have withstood the ravages of time. Generally speaking, even purely functional household textiles seem to have survived in excellent condition in relatively affluent Lancaster County households. As one studies household inventories of the late 1800s and early 1900s, old family household sales, and collections still remaining in early homes, textiles seem to abound in direct proportion to the family's affluence.

The Hearts pattern quilt (fig. 52) was probably made by Barbara Charles (Mrs. Jacob) Seitz. The Seitz family members were affluent Mennonite farmers living in the Central Manor area of Manor Township. As they were successful farmers living in a highly productive part of the county, it is not surprising that the family retained a number of other mid-nineteenth century plain and decorative household linens and bedcoverings along with the quilt. Although the concept is simple, a white ground with only hearts appliqued as decoration, the layout, difficulty of execution, and iconography make the bedcover an appropriate presentation piece for a new arrival.

A more elaborately appliqued Sampler crib quilt (fig. 53) is one of two almost identical quilts made by Lizzie Kulp Buch of Akron for her daughters, Bertha and Erla. Lizzie, a member of the Church of the Brethren, made the piece around 1901 for the birth of daughter Bertha.

Lizzie's family were active quiltmakers, and she had quilts prepared before her marriage to Aaron Wenger Buch on September 25, 1888. A wedding photograph (fig. 54) shows the couple at the bride's home. The Buch family was prosperous, and Aaron became a farmer and botanist; he was active in church affairs and was a founder of the Brownstown bank. Lizzie made many other quilts for special events such as births, marriages, and graduations, a tradition that is continued today by the women of her family.

Hannah K. Blank Zook, an Old Order Amish woman, pieced the Sunshine and Shadows pattern crib quilt (fig. 55) for her son Daniel, who was born in 1933. Hannah was the wife of David K. Zook, a farmer living near Intercourse in Leacock Township. As with most Lancaster Amish quilts, there are no printed fabrics in her work. Using cotton shirting material she had on hand, Hannah intended the quilt for use; but even after many washings, when her children were grown, she saved it as a keepsake.

Fig. 52
Hearts crib quilt, four-block pattern using single heart motif as basic design element. Attributed to Mennonite maker Barbara Charles (Mrs. Jacob) Seitz 1808-48), Manor Township, c. 1840. Appliqued cotton top, cotton batting, cotton back, 37" x 39". *Private collection.*

Left:
Fig. 53
Sampler crib quilt made for Bertha Buch at her birth by her mother Lizzie, who made a similar piece for another daughter, Erla. Maker was Lizzie Kulp Buch (1866-1939), Akron Borough, 1901. Appliqued and pieced cotton top, cotton batting, cotton back. 41" square. *Private collection*.

Above: Fig. 54
Lizzie Kulp Buch (1866-1939), maker of Sampler crib quilt (fig. 53), and Aaron Wenger Buch (1866-1948), Akron Borough, on occasion of their marriage, September 25, 1888. *Image courtesy of Mr. and Mrs. Lester Davidson.*

Fig. 55
Sunshine and Shadows crib quilt made from scraps of shirting material for Daniel Zook, Old Order Amish boy, by his mother Hannah Zook (1900-86), Leacock Township, 1933. Pieced cotton top, cotton batting, cotton back, 46.5" square. *Private collection*.

CHILDHOOD

Childhood, as a stage in life, is celebrated in many ways by parents and grandparents worldwide. Creating toys, dolls, and doll quilts was common practice in southeastern Pennsylvania. The bedding and bedstead combination (fig. 56) made for Eliza (Lizzie) Hershey Zug was a joint effort by her grandparents John and Eliza Graybill Hershey. They were members of the Church of the Brethren and lived in Mastersonville. Grandfather Hershey lovingly crafted the tiny bed to which Lizzie's grandmother Eliza added the bedding. The set is a miniature representation of a Pennsylvania German bed and bedstead (fig. 6), complete with straw mattress, bolster covered with handsewn linens, and a Nine Patch pattern quilt.

Examples of two other doll quilts (figs. 57 and 59) were saved by their owners long after dolls and other playthings had been cast aside. The first one is a Postage Stamp variation called Trip around the World by Mennonite quilters. It belonged to Lizzie M. Bomberger, a Mennonite woman from Elm, Penn Township. According to family history, it was made sometime in the early 1900s.

Left:
Fig. 56
Doll bed and bedding made for Lizzie Hershey Zug (1895-1973), Church of the Brethren child. Miniature rendition of traditional Pennsylvania German bed and bedding, made by grandparents John Hershey and Eliza Graybill Hershey (dates unknown), Rapho Township, c. 1900. Quilt: pieced cotton top, cotton batting, cotton back, 14.5" square; bedding: cotton and straw; bed: painted softwood, 15.25" x 11" x 8/5". *Collection of Susan Patton Munn.*

Above: Fig. 57
Trip around the World doll quilt owned and attributed to Mennonite girl, Lizzie M. Bomberger (1893-1987), Penn Township, c. 1900. Pieced cotton top, machine quilting, cotton batting, cotton back, 17.25" square. *Private collection.*

Left:
Fig. 58
Phares and Fanny Bomberger family, c. 1905, showing on far right Lizzie M. Bomberger (1893-1987), owner of Trip around the World doll quilt (fig. 57). The Bombergers were owners of the village store in Pennville [now Elm], still in business today. *Image courtesy of Arlene M. Eby.*

Below:
Fig. 59
Nine Block doll quilt owned and possibly made by Amish girl Mary M. Lapp (1920-) and her mother Lavinia Miller Lapp (1885-1950), Lancaster Township, 1927. Pieced cotton top, cotton batting, cotton back, 14" x 15". *Private collection.*

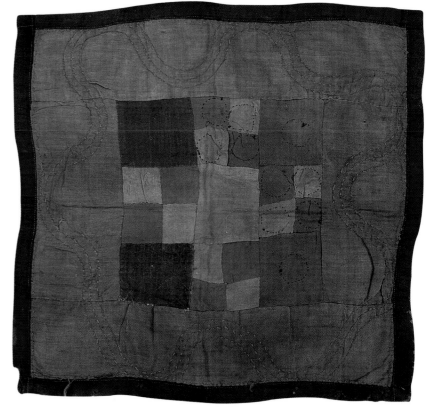

Lizzie is seen with her family in a photograph (fig. 58) taken when she was about twelve years old, showing her parents, sister, and three of her four brothers. Lizzie's parents, Phares and Fanny Bomberger, were storekeepers in the small village of Pennville (now Elm), in Penn Township. Lizzie, who never married, spent many years working as a missionary in Miner's Village, Lebanon County, before coming home to live with her mother and sister Katie.[8] The Bomberger women were known as active quilters, and, according to family members, they kept a quilting frame set up in a spare room upstairs. It almost always held a quilt waiting to be finished. No doubt Lizzie treasured the little quilt, because it survived with few signs of wear before being sold at her estate auction almost fifty years later.

A pieced doll quilt (fig. 59) belonged to Lancaster Amish girl Mary Lapp, who later became the second wife of Christian E. Stoltzfus. Mary made the quilt with the help of her mother, Lavinia Miller Lapp, in the mid-1920s when she was five or six years old. The coarse and uneven stitching and piecing suggests that this may have been one of her first sewing projects. Although it was heavily used and repeatedly washed, Mary kept it for about fifty years before parting with it.

DOWRY

Making quilts for a daughter or son in preparation for marriage was standard procedure for most southeastern Pennsylvania households.[9] Many quilts were made as the children were growing up, often with help from other members of the family and close friends. They usually accumulated within a dower chest (fig. 60) until the daughter or son was married. The inscription inside the lid indicates that this chest was made for Ida Snyder Stoner in 1911.

Ida's quilt (fig. 61) was stored in her dower chest until her marriage to Reuben Sweigart Horst on November 12, 1914. The quilt was made by her mother Barbara Snyder Stoner sometime around 1895 and was often referred to by the family as the Puzzle quilt. The pieces, barely one inch square, are arranged in a block construction that collectors refer to as Philadelphia Pavement. Barbara and her husband John M. Stoner were Mennonites who farmed near the village of Merrill in Ephrata Township. Ida recollected that her quilt must have been made before she was ten years old or she would have helped her mother work on it.

Barbara and Ida appear with their family and friends in photographs of a quilting party, (figs. 216 and 217). From the photographs it appears that the whole family enjoyed quiltmaking and its social aspects. Family members say that Barbara sometimes dyed fabrics to get shades she wanted to use for quilts. Barbara made many quilts, but most of them were used and thrown away or recycled for use inside comforters. What she considered her best quilt was her most elaborate, and it was never used (fig. 218). Barbara seems to have enjoyed the challenge of working with small pieces.

Fig. 60
Dower chest used to store dowry quilt (fig. 61) and other items put away for marriage by Ida Snyder Stoner (1891-1978), East Earl Township. Her name and date, "Ida S. Stoner/1911," are painted on underside of lid. Maker unknown, 1911. Grain-painted and varnished poplar, 38" x 21" x 23.75". *Collection of Sheryl Quickel.*

Fig. 61
Philadelphia Pavement
or Puzzle quilt, as it was
known to the Stoner
family, made for Ida
Snyder Stoner (1891-
1987) by her mother
Barbara Snyder Stoner
(1862-1922), East Earl
Township, c. 1895.
Pieced cotton top,
cotton batting, cotton
back, 84" x 82". *Collection of Clarke E. Hess.*

MARRIAGE

Less commonly, a quilt would be made for the specific event of a marriage (figs. 37 and 62). Of the 884 quilts documented during the initial Quilt Harvest days, 210 quilts—almost one-quarter—were known to have been made for a special life event. Seventy five percent of the latter group were made for a dowry (going into housekeeping) or an actual marriage. Detailed information on quilts made for rites of passage is extracted from Quilt Harvest data (fig. 63).

Fanny Gish and John L. Shot received an album quilt at the time of their wedding in 1854, perhaps because Fanny was raised as an orphan. Their quilt (figs. 37 and 62) bears the signatures of many friends and neighbors from the Manheim area, who probably made a communal effort to see that Fanny was properly prepared for marriage. Born in the late 1890s, Fanny was left in Lebanon County by her father to be raised by another family after her mother died. Family tradition says that she was so poor that as a child she never owned a pair of shoes and, later in her life, expressed a wish to be buried with her shoes on when she died. It is unlikely she would have been able to bring several quilts to her marriage as the traditional dowry.

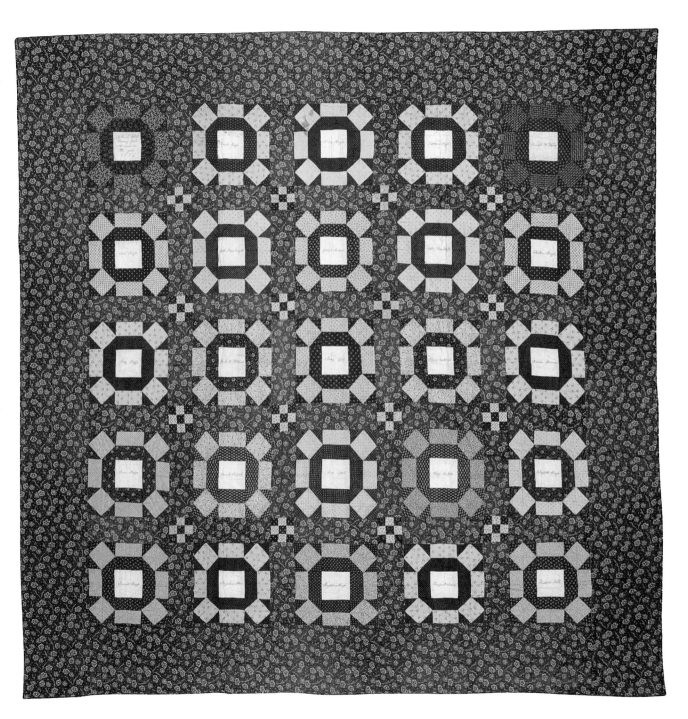

Fig. 62
Signature Marriage quilt made for marriage of John L. Shot (189?-?) and Fanny Gish (189?-?), Rapho Township, 1854. Left upper corner block (fig. 37) records couple's names and date. Pieced cotton top, signatures in running stitch, cotton batting, cotton backing, 90" square. *Heritage Center of Lancaster County through the generosity of the James Hale Steinman Foundation.*

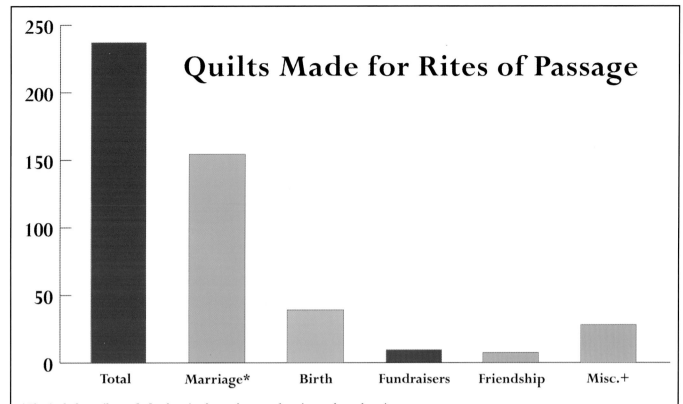

Quilts Made for Rites of Passage

*Also includes quilts made for dowries, hope chests, and setting up housekeeping
+Quilts made for birthdays, departures, and other miscellaneous events

Left:
Fig. 63
Statistical analysis of quilts made for family rites of passage, using information gathered from Heritage Center of Lancaster County Quilt Harvest data recorded in 1988 and 1989.

Below:
Fig. 64
Memorial doll quilt quilted in blue thread with the inscription, "A gift from Ann Elisabeth Witmer to Ann Elisabeth Brubaker 1843/Born 1839 Died 1843/Aged 13 years 7 months 6 days," indicating that it was made to commemorate the death of Ann Elisabeth Brubaker (1839-43). The "Aged 13 years 7 months 6 days" refers to the maker's age. Ann Elisabeth Witmer (c.1830-?), New Providence Township, 1843. Pieced cotton top, cotton batting, cotton back. 16" x 18.5". *Private collection.*

DEATH

The small quilt (fig. 64) is a poignant reminder of the final rite of passage—death. The white strips and outer borders are the only quilted areas. The blue running-stitch quilting is done in lines of script that read: "A gift from Ann Elisabeth Witmer to Ann Elisabeth Brubaker 1843/Born 1839 Died 1843/Aged 13 years 7 months 6 days." This is likely the oldest dated Lancaster County doll-size quilt known, and perhaps the only one done as a memorial to a child. Ann, the maker, was the daughter of John and Anna Brubaker Witmer of New Providence in southern Lancaster County.[10] Nothing is known about four-year-old Ann Elisabeth Brubaker, who may have been her namesake. Although small in size, the memorial is an unusually sophisticated piece for a girl thirteen and a half years old to have created; it survives as a memorial to this small child.

Because of the stability and affluence of the Lancaster County population, a large proportion of these special quilts have survived and often remain in the families for which they were made. This allows us to appreciate the special relationship quilts have within the social structure of the residents of Lancaster County.

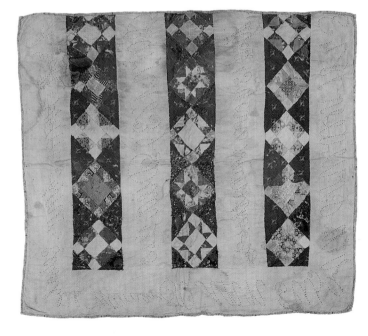

Chapter Four

CHURCH, MISSION, AND COMMUNITY:
Fundraiser Quilts

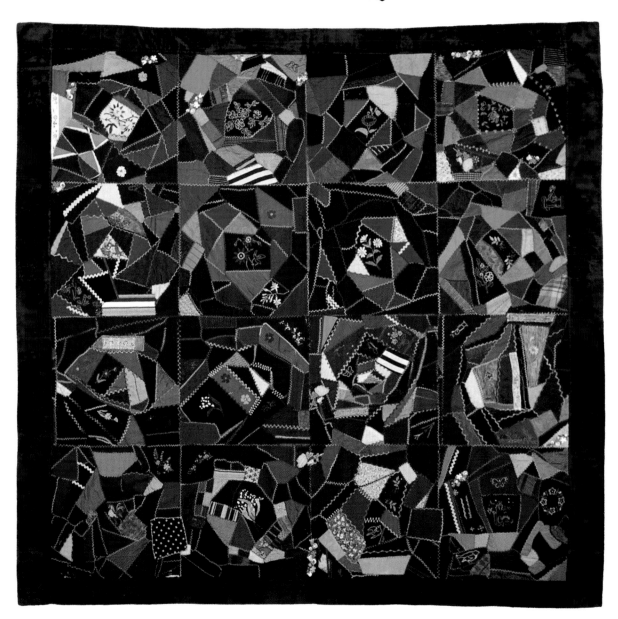

Fig. 65
Crazy quilt made as a gift to a missionary, the Rev. John F. Musselman (1878-1947), and his wife Alice Daugherty Musselman (dates unknown) in Sierra Leone, West Africa, by Woman's Missionary Society of Covenant Evangelical United Brethren (now Covenant United Methodist) Church, Lancaster City, c.1915. Pieced cotton, silk, and silk velvet top, no quilting or batting, cotton back, 78" x 81". *Collection of Covenant United Methodist Church.*

"Go ye into all the world and preach the Gospel to every creature." The passage from Mark 16:18 is written on a back border of a Crazy quilt (fig. 65). A detail (fig. 66) shows the "cheater's cloth," or faux quilt print used for part of the backing. Extensive writing on the border areas indicates that the quilt was made by the Woman's Missionary Society of Covenant United Brethren Church of Lancaster (now Covenant United Methodist Church) as a gift for the Rev. John F. Musselman, pastor, in Sierra Leone, West Africa.

Along with this information are the names of almost 350 people, members of the missionary society and the church. Probably each person paid a sum of money for the listing, and the money was then used to support missionary work in Sierra Leone. Covenant Church had special concern for John Musselman (fig. 67), as he had become a member of that congregation when he was eighteen years old. Mrs. Musselman, the former Alice Daugherty of Lebanon County, Pennsylvania, began missionary work in Africa in 1907, the year before Rev.

Fig. 67
Rev. John F. Musselman (1878-1947) and wife Alice Daugherty Musselman (dates unknown), missionaries in Sierra Leone, West Africa, for whom a fundraiser Crazy quilt (fig. 65) was made. The couple was supported by the congregation of Covenant Evangelical United Brethren (now Covenant United Methodist) Church, Lancaster City, 1911-20. *Image courtesy of Covenant United Methodist Church.*

Fig. 66
Detail of back of Crazy quilt (fig. 65) showing "cheater's cloth" or faux quilt print, a simulation of a pieced Crazy quilt design, c. 1915. Pieced cotton, silk, and silk velvet top, no quilting or batting, cotton back, 78" x 81". *Collection of Covenant United Methodist Church.*

Musselman arrived. During his first furlough they returned to Pennsylvania to be married. Their work continued there until 1947, totally supported by funds from Covenant Church. Rev. Musselman died suddenly on a Sunday morning three months after his return to the United States.

The quilt was made sometime between 1911 and 1920, during the time the Rev. G. D. Batdorf was pastor in Lancaster, as his name appears among those on the back of the quilt. The process of making the quilt, raising money, and sending the quilt to their own missionary in a far-off land further reinforced the close bonds and missionary zeal the congregation held for their missionaries and mission in Africa. The Musselmans kept the quilt in Sierra Leone while they were there. It was returned to the church in 1950 and rediscovered in 1990 in time to be included in the Heritage Center Quilt Harvest project. It is now exhibited on special mission days at what is now Covenant United Methodist Church and continues to reinforce the congregation's interest in missionary work.

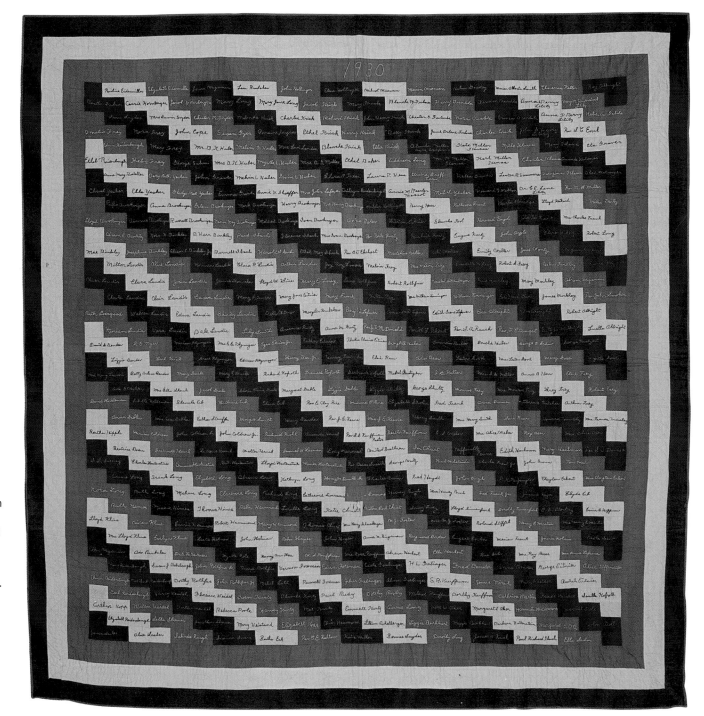

Fig. 68
Diagonal Block Signature Fundraiser quilt made by Ladies Aid Society of Long Memorial United Brethren (now United Methodist) Church, Neffsville, Manheim Township, quilted by a member, Annie Landis Long (1889-1998). Her husband Franklin purchased it as an additional way to raise money for the church, 1930. Pieced cotton top, woven cotton gauze filling, cotton back, 75" square. *Collection of Long Memorial United Methodist Church.*

Fig. 69
Double Irish Chain Signature Fundraiser quilt made by the Woman's Missionary Society of the First Presbyterian Church, whose ability to squeeze in many signatures was astounding; Lancaster City, 1934-35. Pieced cotton top with outline stitch embroidery of donors' names, woven flannel filling, cotton back, 103.5" x 93". *Collection of First Presbyterian Church, Lancaster, Pennsylvania.*

A bright red, yellow, and green embroidered Diagonal Block quilt (fig. 68) is a purely Pennsylvania interpretation of a church fundraising quilt. A note attached gives the history of the quilt:

Note—1930 Quilt

This quilt was a project of the Ladies Aid Society of the Long Memorial United Brethren Church (now United Methodist) of Neffsville, Pa. For a donation of 10 cents a member or friend or relative could have their name embroidered on one of the patches of the quilt.

The embroidery work was done by various members of the Society. Sewing the top together, assembling the quilt, and the actual quilting was done by another member, Annie L. Long. The quilt was eventually sold and was bought by Mrs. Long's husband, Franklin B. Long.

Annie and her husband Franklin were farmers and members of the church. She was known for her quilting, which she did in her spare time when her quilting frame was set up in her living room or bedroom. Another example of Annie's work (fig. 150) is also known. The fundraising quilt raised money not only with each signature donation but also with the money Franklin paid to buy it when it was completed. In 1982 the quilt came back to the church as a donation from Mrs. Long. In 1988 Annie passed away at the age of ninety-nine, leaving this bright and joyful piece as her legacy.

By choosing a red, green, and yellow palette the women left no doubt in later observers' minds that this is a southeastern Pennsylvania quilt. Using only the three classic-colored blocks, repeating them as borders, and alternating the same colors of embroidery thread so the names contrast on the blocks, produces a startling statement. This is hardly the quiet reserved object one might expect to have been made in the 1930s within the confines of a church.

The ladies of the First Presbyterian Church Womans Missionary Society used another variation of pieced work (fig. 69) to induce members and friends to donate money. They chose the more traditional Irish Chain pattern, reserving the white areas for names. The palette is similar to Long Memorial's quilt, but the fabrics are small prints instead of solid-colored cottons. The names placed with red embroidery are arranged in a variety of innovative ways.

In a block just above the center of the quilt red outline stitching reads:

This quilt made
by
Womans Missionary Society
First Presbyterian Church
Lancaster Pa.
1934-1935

The outcome of this kind of church project accomplished several things: raising money for a worthy cause, bonding of church members, involvement of community, and heightened awareness of the church and its mission. Present-day Mennonite women are pictured (fig. 70) holding a quilting bee in Martindale, Pennsylvania. The quilt they are working on was then sold at the world-famous Mennonite Relief Sale held every spring in Harrisburg, to raise funds for world-wide Mennonite mission work. This activity, a common practice throughout the United States, is alive and well in modern-day Lancaster County.

Fig. 70
Mennonite women, Martindale, Lancaster County, preparing a quilt for donation to annual Mennonitie Relief Sale held in Harrisburg, Pennsylvania, c. 1995. *Image courtesy of Pennsylvania Dutch Convention & Visitors Bureau. Photograph by Keith Baum.*

Chapter Five

THE QUAKER INFLUENCE

The name Pennsylvania, translated as "Penn's Woods," conjures up a picture of idyllic wooded lands settled by early followers of English Quaker William Penn. One can imagine these men and women in plain dress, living in peaceful close-knit communities in the fertile valleys of Pennsylvania. Their life style has been typified by the quote "of the best Sort but Plain."[11]

Quakers, officially known as the Religious Society of Friends, first arrived in the American Colonies in 1656. They set up Meetings of Worship—the basic unit of the organization—in Rhode Island, Massachusetts, and Maryland. Because of continued persecution in their native England, large numbers of Quakers began to emigrate through the port of Philadelphia in 1682. By 1700 Quaker settlements were located along the Atlantic seaboard throughout Rhode Island, Massachusetts, New York, Pennsylvania, Maryland, Virginia, and North Carolina. Once they had settled in the Philadelphia area, it is not surprising that large numbers of Quakers spread into what is now southeastern Lancaster County, in the area bordering the more heavily Quaker-settled Chester County.[12]

To describe Lancaster Quaker quilts as being "of the best Sort but Plain" is an oversimplification. Like other Pennsylvania Quaker quilts, they were made from the highest quality fabrics—frequently silk dress materials used by Quaker women. Because the silks were often soft solid greys and browns and small-scale prints, one might consider them plain. Whether made of cotton or silk, the pieced quilts were frequently of a block design consisting of many small pieces. The piecing usually appears to have been well-planned and meticulously executed. This is consistent with the English template method of piecing (Fig 15). Those Quaker quilts that were appliqued were also based on a block design using small-scale printed fabrics. For the most part the color juxtaposition and elaborate nature of the patterns and embellishments found in Lancaster Quaker pieced and appliqued quilts challenge the designation "Plain."

The earliest quilts documented in Pennsylvania are Whole-Cloth silk quilts (fig. 2) made and owned by Quakers living in the middle of the 1700s in the Philadelphia area. Although no quilts of that period have been found in Lancaster County, local examples from the middle of the 1800s closely resemble quilts being made by members of the Philadelphia and Burlington, New Jersey, meetings. It is not surprising that the majority of Lancaster Quaker quilts were made by families living in southeastern Lancaster County, the area closest to Philadelphia.

The oldest surviving Lancaster County Quaker quilt (fig. 71), according to family history, was made by Deborah Simmons Coates shortly after her marriage to Lindley Coates in 1819. A detail of a central triangle in the quilt (fig. 72) reveals the stamped figure of a slave. Similar images were used by a number of anti-slavery organizations in the early 1800s. Deborah's husband Lindley, like many other Quakers at that time, was active in the abolition movement. He served as president of the American Anti-Slavery Society in 1840. The Coates home, located near Christiana, Sadsbury Township, was station number five on the Underground Railroad in Lancaster County.[13] It is apparent that Deborah shared strong anti-slavery convictions with her husband.

Another type of quilt frequently made by Quaker women was the Friendship or Signature quilt. The popularity of this type of quilt in Quaker settlements hints at the strong sense of community present among the Quakers. The Papercut Friendship appliqued quilt top (fig. 73) was apparently assembled by Lydia A. Bradley and descended in her family. The family always called it the Friendship quilt. Names of friends from Drumore and Fulton Townships are written in ink on the individual blocks with dates ranging from 1845 through 1847. A detail (fig. 39) shows the signature of the likely maker, Lydia Bradley. The blocks were not joined together immediately, as the sashing between the squares is of a later date. It remains in an unfinished state with no filling, back, or quilting. The materials selected are a variety of high-quality printed red cottons on a white ground. These fabrics and this design were particularly popular in the 1840s in Lancaster families of English descent. Similar quilts (figs. 118, 120, and 121) are discussed in the chapter on Papercut quilts.

Pieced block patterns are the most frequently occurring among Quaker quilts in Lancaster County. Two examples (figs. 74 and 76) were made by members of the Lamborn family, who lived near the Drumore and Martic Township border. Ann Ambler Lamborn is believed to have made a Star

Fig. 71
Triangle quilt pieced using template method, made of high-quality dress silks typical of Quaker quilting done in early to mid-1800s. Small central white cotton triangle printed with slave image. Quilt was cut down the middle into two pieces through the image so it could be given to two descendants. Made by Deborah Simmons Coates (born c. 1800-1888), Sadsbury Township, 1820s. Pieced silk and cotton top, cotton batting, cotton back, 89" x 95". *Heritage Center of Lancaster County through the generosity of Marjorie A. Laidman.*

Block quilt (fig. 74). A note previously attached to it mentions that the quilt was made sometime before 1861. Ann (fig. 75) was the wife of Aquilla Bolton Lamborn, a Quaker farmer in the area of Wentz's Mill.

A silk quilt (fig. 76) was pieced from mid-1800s silk dress fabrics anchored with simple waffle pattern quilting. It is attributed to Addie Lamborn (fig. 77), the daughter of Ann and Aquilla, and was made for Addie's grandnephew Howard Long. She was crippled by a spinal abnormality, never married, and became a professional seamstress. She traveled from place to place, living with various families and making clothing for them. She may have saved scraps from dresses she produced to make her bedcovering.

Marianna Gibbons Brubaker, an affluent Quaker lady living at the family farm, Beechdale, near Bird-In-Hand, Upper Leacock Township, gives us a day-by-day diary description of work on her two silk quilts. The silk bedcoverings (figs. 78 and 80), which she called her Hexagonal and Octagonal quilts, were completed in 1892 and 1894.

Born in 1848, Marianna did more than make quilts. The daughter of a doctor, she attended college and was a writer, housewife, and temperance lecturer. In 1892, at the age of 56, about the time she was making her quilts, Marianna married Orem David (O.D.) Brubaker. He was a farmer and 40-year-old widower with nine children, ranging in age from two to sixteen. The couple, committed to the abolitionist movement, were acquainted with Lindley and Deborah Coates, the owners of the first Quaker quilt pictured in this chapter (fig. 71). It is amazing that Marianna was able to persevere with her quiltmaking, considering her new duties as a wife and stepmother.

The following are a few of the many notations from a diary kept in the third person by Marianna and her sister Caro (Caroline), recording work being done on the Hexagonal quilt (fig. 78). Written mostly by Marianna, it provides us with a verbal picture of her on-and-off quiltmaking techniques:

Fig. 72
Detail of Triangle quilt (fig. 71), showing slave image and the words "Deliver me from the oppression/of man." Its maker's husband was Lindley Coates, a Quaker active in the abolitionist movement. Coates's home was Station #5 on the Underground Railroad. Made by Deborah Simmons Coates (born c. 1800-1888), Sadsbury Township, 1820s. Pieced silk top, cotton batting, cotton back, 89" x 95". *Heritage Center of Lancaster County through the generosity of Marjorie A. Laidman.*

Friday, February 6, 1891
M. [Marianna] brings down her silk pieces in the afternoon and begins preparing to make a silk quilt.

Thursday, November 13, 1891
M. is very busy, ripping old silk dress waists for pieces for a silk quilt which she has decided to begin.

Saturday, November 14, 1891
M. busy pressing her silks and cutting some out and putting them together in "patches".
Saturday, December 12, 1891

Fig. 73
Papercut Friendship quilt top, the centers of each block signed with friends' and neighbors' names from the area surrounding the owner's southern Lancaster County home. Lydia's name is signed in two blocks with the dates 1846 and 1848 (fig. 39). Pieced with sashing at a later date. Attributed to Lydia A. Bradley (dates unknown), Drumore or Fulton Township, 1845-47. Appliqued and pieced top, 70" square.
Collection of Gloria S. Smith.

Left:
Fig. 74
Star Block quilt, had note previously attached saying it was made by Quakeress Ann Ambler (Mrs. Aquilla) Lamborn (1831-94), Drumore Township, before 1860. Pieced cotton top, cotton batting, cotton back, 98" square. *Collection of Mitchell K. Long.*

Below:
Fig. 75
Ann Lamborn (1831-1894), photograph probably taken in 1870s. She was maker of Star Block quilt (fig. 74) and was the wife of Aquilla Lamborn, farmer at Wentz's Mill in southern Lancaster County. *Image courtesy of Mitchell K. Long.*

Left:
Fig. 76
Block quilt made by professional seamstress Addie Lamborn. She was the daughter of the previously noted quiltmaker Ann Lamborn. Silks may have been dress scraps she saved. Gift for grandnephew Howard Long from Addie Lamborn (1875-1926), Drumore Township, c. 1850. Pieced silk top, cotton batting, cotton back, 70" square. *Collection of Marshall Long.*

Below:
Fig. 77
Addie Lamborn (1875-1926), Drumore Township, maker of Block quilt (fig. 76). Addie, standing on crutches in the center of the group, was crippled by a spinal abnormality; she never married and became a professional seamstress, 1916. *Image courtesy of Marshall Long.*

In the afternoon she [Marianna's sister Caro] goes to the village [Bird-in-Hand] to get the things from Philadelphia. Among them is a box of silk and velvet pieces for M. from Miss Dimond—a very nice thing as some of them are beautiful. M. sews a good deal.

Thursday, December 17, 1891
M. busy pressing the pieces that Miss Dimond sent her—also nine beautiful pieces sent by Mr. John D. Bowen's a day or two ago.

Wednesday, March 9, 1892
M. finished the last patch of her silk quilt which she began 11 mo. 14, 1891 she has made all 37 patches, one being unfit, she gave to Mabel [the young daughter of the farm manager]

Friday, March 11, 1892
M. begins the work of putting her quilt together.

Thursday, August 11, 1892
M. and Mrs. Buch arrange about the latter's finishing and quilting the quilt that M. began under our dear grandmother's supervision, so many years ago.

Wednesday, November 22, 1893
M. begins again, on her silk quilt, hoping to finish it this time.

Saturday, December 9, 1893
This evening M. finished her silk quilt which she began more than two years ago. She did not however work on it last winter.[14]

A detail photograph of a back corner of the Hexagonal quilt (fig. 79) reveals a handwritten cloth label attached by Marianna Gibbons Brubaker in 1921. It reads:

The wool with which this quilt is filled was the filling of an old fashioned "comfort" that belonged to my beloved grandmother, Hannah W. Gibbons (1787-1850). When It was begun, my dear Sister, Caroline Gibbons (1848-1900) suggested that I should use this wool as a filling for it. In the hope that the example of these two noble good women may be followed by her, this quilt is given to my precious daughter Elisabeth on her wedding day by her loving mother. Sept 3, 1921. M.G.B.

"My precious daughter Elisabeth" refers to her stepdaughter, one of the children of O. D. Brubaker, whom Marianna obviously loved as if she were her own child. So a cherished memory of a grandmother was added to a quilt worked on in Marianna's single days, shared with her beloved sister Caroline. The quilt then became a special gift laden with memories of past generations and presented to a daughter on her wedding day.

Not deterred by the long fitful process of making the Hexagonal quilt, Marianna started another quilt on December 18, 1894. The top to the Octagonal quilt (figs. 80 and 81) was speedily completed on March 26, 1895 with the diary notation "This evening M. finishes the twenty-fourth patch of her silk quilt, being the last except the center one which is to be embroidered."[15] A detail (fig. 81) reveals the letters "MG" in the central octagon surrounded by octagons embroidered with branching white flowers.

The most recently produced Quaker quilt (fig. 82) among those studied was made by Roberta Penrose Carrigan. She was the daughter of Benjamin and Hannah Lukens Penrose, descendants of Welsh immigrants living in Bucks County. She married Enos Carrigan, of Irish descent, a farmer and investor residing in Drumore Township. The quilt was made there in about 1920. A studio photograph of Roberta (fig. 83) was taken at about the same time. She is pictured wearing a stylishly tailored dress as her granddaughter remembers was typical of Roberta.

Of all the quilts illustrated, Roberta's quilt appears to uphold the concept of plain Quaker life best. It is a simple Four Patch quilt, using small-print cottons throughout. The Carrigans were prosperous people and could well afford fine-quality fabrics, which these appear to be. At least one other quilt made by Roberta was made from silks, but it does not survive.

Although Quaker quilts cannot be narrowly defined and limited to only the few specific types mentioned here, they often contain clues to their origin. Whole cloth silk quilts made in the 1700s might possibly be found in Lancaster County and would most likely be Quaker bedcoverings. Quilts made during the 1800s, containing high-quality dress silks, and meticulous piecing, using the English template method, also suggest a Quaker provenance. In the later 1800s and early 1900s small-print expensive cotton materials were also likely to have been used by Quaker quiltmakers.

Left:
Fig. 78
Hexagonal quilt started in 1891, top completed in 1893, documented in diary kept by the maker, well-to-do Quakeress Marianna Gibbons (Mrs. Orem David) Brubaker (1848-1929), Upper Leacock Township, 1891-93. Pieced silk top, wool batting, cotton back, 67" x 63". *Collection of Mr. and Mrs. John Salzmann.*

Below:
Fig. 79
Detail of back corner label noting gift to adopted daughter Elisabeth, sewn on Hexagonal quilt (fig. 78) by maker Marianna Gibbons (Mrs. Orem David) Brubaker (1848-1929), Upper Leacock Township, 1891-93. Pieced silk top, wool batting, cotton back , 67" x 63". *Collection of Mr. and Mrs. John Salzmann.*

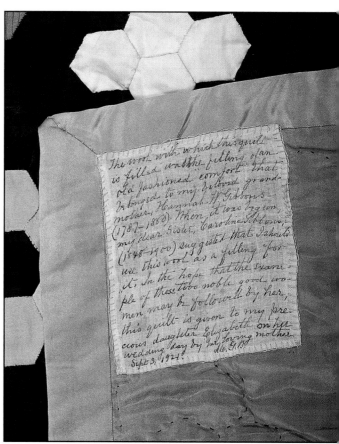

Right:
Fig. 80
Octagonal quilt by same maker who made Hexagonal quilt (fig. 78). This Octagonal quilt is also mentioned in its maker's diary as being finished the following year, 1894. Batting and backing added later, Marianna Gibbons (Mrs. Orem David) Brubaker (1848-1929), Upper Leacock Township, 1891-93. Pieced silk top, cotton batting, cotton back, 58" square. *Collection of Marian Brubaker.*

Below:
Fig. 81
Detail of center block of Octagonal quilt (fig. 80), mentioned by maker in her diary on March 26, 1895. Marianna Gibbons Brubaker (1848-1929), Upper Leacock Township, 1891-93. Pieced silk top, cotton batting, cotton back, 58" square. *Collection of Marian Brubaker.*

Left:
Fig. 82
Four Block quilt made by Quaker woman of Welsh descent, Roberta Penrose (Mrs. Enos) Carrigan (1854-1942), Drumore Township, c. 1920. Pieced cotton top, cotton batting, cotton back, 77" square. *Collection of Roselyn C. Dommel.*

Below:
Fig. 83
Roberta Penrose (Mrs. Enos) Carrigan (1854-1942), Drumore Township, c. 1895, maker of Four Block quilt (fig. 82). Roberta is seated in the front row, far left, beside her youngest children, Lester and Grace. Husband Enos and son Harry are next. In the back row are daughters Rena and Learia. *Image courtesy of Roselyn C. Dommel.*

Chapter Six
AMISH QUILTS

LANCASTER COUNTY! THE AMISH! QUILTS! These are almost involuntary word associations made by anyone with some knowledge of southeastern Pennsylvania. Because the Amish people are easily identified visually and seem to be surrounded by a mystique that appeals to visitors, they have an obvious value to the tourist industry (fig. 84). The same mystique and the easily identifiable characteristics of their quilts have endeared their bedcoverings to the quilt collecting community, too.

Roots of the Amish religion go back to the Protestant Reformation when, in 1525, the Anabaptists—those believing in adult baptism—gathered in Zurich, Switzerland. In the late 1600s a group led by Jakob Ammann broke away from the established church and the movement separated into two distinct groups, the Amish and the Mennonites. The first Amish families to arrive in Lancaster County were the members of two congregations who settled the region in about 1790. The community remained small—fewer than 500 people—until the early twentieth century, but it is the oldest Amish settlement in continuous existence. There are now almost 250 Amish settlements in twenty-two states. Today the Lancaster Amish community numbers more than 20,000 and is second only to the Holmes County, Ohio, settlement in population.[16] As

Fig. 84
A typical picturesque view of an Amish farm in Lancaster County, Pennsylvania, an area visited by six million tourists a year. Familiarity with the outer visages of Amish life increases awareness the general public has in all things Amish. Interest in antique quilts made by the Lancaster Amish community has been directly affected by this general awareness of the group's lifestyle. *Image courtesy of the Pennsylvania Dutch Convention & Visitors Bureau, Lancaster, Pennsylvania. Photograph by Ron Bowman.*

one of the earliest and most active Amish settlements, the Lancaster Amish community has continued to hold the interest of scholars and collectors.[17]

Because the Amish have chosen to remain a cohesive group and maintain a separation from the surrounding community—more than other religious groups such as the Mennonites or Quakers—their decorative arts also have evolved in a more isolated environment. As a result, the quilts produced for use within their own community have certain characteristics that identify them easily, not simply as Amish, but as Lancaster Amish. They are visually different from quilts made by their Lancaster neighbors and by other Amish settlements. But like the other Pennsylvania Germans in Lancaster County, early Amish settlers were more likely to have used coverlets as bedcoverings and adapted to the use of quilts only later in the 1800s.

By examining a variety of local Amish quilts made during the first half of the twentieth century, one can recognize the hallmarks of traditional quiltmaking within the community. It also may be possible to determine what effect outside influences have had on Lancaster Amish quiltmakers and, conversely, whether Amish quiltmakers have in any way brought changes to quilts being made by their neighbors.

Fig. 85
Sunshine and Shadows quilt,
pattern associated with later
1930s through present day,
now the most popular of
traditional patterns still being
made by local Amish women
for themselves. The maker is
a member of the King family,
Lancaster County, 1945-55.
Pieced wool, cotton and
rayon top, cotton batting,
cotton back, 80" square.
*Heritage Center of Lancaster
County through the generosity of D. Curry Pettus.
Photograph by Charles
Studio of Photography.*

Three patterns immediately come to mind when one thinks of Lancaster Amish quilts: Sunshine and Shadows (fig. 85), Center Diamond (fig. 86), and Bars (fig. 87). In that order, these quilts appear to have been the most popular with Amish quiltmakers during the first half of the twentieth century. Most valued by collectors today are quilts of the Center Diamond pattern. Because of this selection process, they appear to make up a higher percentage of surviving quilts in private collections and museums than the ratio of quilts actually produced. (Sunshine and Shadows quilts were probably the most popular with Amish women.) The majority of Sunshine and Shadows designs are later quilts made in the 1940s and 1950s. Contemporary with the Center Diamond, but less frequently found, are the Bars quilts.

The classic Center Diamond (fig. 86), in a single image, says "Amish" to most people. Even those not familiar with the intricacies of the art and antiques world have been exposed to the image by some form of marketing. The top is pieced from fine plain-weave wool materials. The quilting patterns, stitched in dark thread, reflect the typical 1920s and 1930s Lancaster Amish quilting vocabulary. The outer borders are done in a feather design, the narrow inner blue borders contain a four-petaled flower within rows of diamond stitching, the purple triangular fields are quilted in a floral and leaf motif, and the red center contains the expected star and feather wreath. As is typical, the middle layer is thin cotton batting, and the back is made from a plain cotton material. The quilt was made for a member of the Benuel King family of southern Lancaster County. Because of its fine and classic patterned quilting and bold-colored wool top, it was probably made in the late 1920s or early 1930s.

During this period Amish quiltmakers were able to purchase materials from an array of sources: nearby dry goods stores in towns such as New Holland and Intercourse, department stores in Lancaster, mail order sources such as the Sears & Roebuck catalogues, and peddlers who came around to the farms with bolts of fabrics and sewing notions in their motor vehicles.[18] When choosing from this variety of sources, women always had an unwritten, unspoken sense as to what fabrics were acceptable within their community.

More evidence that there was a need for community approval comes from comments made by Philadelphia peddler Sam Greenberg's family when interviewed about their business, selling what their advertisements said were "Plain Goods for Plain People." It was the practice of these merchants to load up their automobiles with yard goods bought at bargain rates from New York City and Philadelphia wholesalers, travel west through Pennsylvania, Ohio, and Indiana, and stop at Amish communities along the way. Before visiting the farms they would call upon the bishop of that particular church district and show him any new goods to get approval for use by quilters and seamstresses in that community.[19]

With this in mind one can look at the Bars quilt (fig. 87) and understand the similarity of the fine-weave plain wool fabrics used in the piece with those in the Center Diamond (fig. 86) just discussed. The Bars quilt is signed, in the quilting in a corner near one of the basket handles, "Jessie Bawell" and was likely made for him by his mother Mary Fisher (Mrs. Daniel) Bawell (1879-1946), when Jessie was in his teens. Jessie Bawell (1908-1930) married Rachel Beiler in 1930. The initials "R B" on a back edge of the quilt were probably added by Rachel after their marriage. The majority of Amish quilts were made for children—boys as well as girls—before they were married to "go to housekeeping," a phrase repeatedly used by Pennsylvania German women interviewed for the Quilt Harvest study.

The high quality of the quilting is comparable to that in the Center Diamond, but a less common basket motif is quilted in the outer border. Most Bars quilts have waffle quilting in the central area and this one is no exception. Both quilts have similar quilting patterns in the inner border. Fine workmanship and strong bold-colored wool fabrics, placed so they actively contrast with one another, are key to what attracts collectors to this period in Amish quiltmaking.

The Sunshine and Shadows quilt (fig. 85) represents the most common type made by Lancaster Amish women. A similar pattern, frequently associated with Mennonite quilters, is known as Trip around the World (fig. 148). The Amish example pictured here was probably made sometime between 1945 and 1955. The presence of some cotton and rayon fabrics mixed in with the wools reflects the time period. The outer dark blue border is a rayon blend, nicely quilted in a feather pattern. As would be expected, the center block, or Sunshine and Shadows area, is quilted simply with intersecting parallel lines diagonally across the blocks. The pattern is still used by Amish women in quilts to be set aside for marriage.

A Center Square pattern quilt (fig. 88) is one of the earliest known dated Lancaster Amish quilts. It is simple in design but is embellished with typical feather border quilting patterns with some interesting variations not seen in later examples. The intials "GD" and date "1875" are quilted into one border, and other open areas around the feather quilting are filled with hearts, birds, and tulips. The back is made from solid brown cotton material. Although the center of the quilt is all one fabric, the quilting patterns demarcate a narrow outer border and central blocks on point. The patterns in the blocks alternate between a central star surrounded by a wreath and square grid quilting. The quilting patterns seem to emulate block quilts being made by non-Amish neighbors. There is also a similarity to the block patterns occasionally used by Lancaster Amish women

Fig. 86
Center Diamond quilt, with red center, fine quilting, and uncluttered design, considered by collectors as a classic Lancaster County Amish quilt design. Made by a member of the Benuel King family, southern Lancaster County, c. 1925. Pieced wool top, cotton batting, cotton back, 75" square. *Heritage Center of Lancaster County through the generosity of the James Hale Steinman Foundation. Photograph by Charles Studio of Photography.*

later in the twentieth century (figs. 89, 90, and, 91).

Besides the actual date and variation in quilting patterns, the fabrics in the quilt are of a slightly finer weave, have a crisper feel, and are less color-saturated than the wools used in twentieth century Amish quilts. It is interesting to note that the seams are joined with machine stitching. Like other active quiltmakers and seamstresses of the period, Amish women were anxious to acquire modern sewing equipment. In the days prior to the electrification of rural homes, which threatened to disrupt the Amish social structure, non-electric appliances that improved the ability of women to produce clothing and quilts were quickly introduced into the home. Rebecca Lapp records in her diary in 1886, "Cloudy all day we sewed morning Lizzie and Mother went to Vogansville to Daniel Weaver for a sewing machine."[20]

Repeated block pattern quilts were less common among Lancaster Amish quilters than the first three central block designs discussed. Even when using repeating blocks, Amish women framed them with prominent, wide, plain, and heavily quilted borders, as seen in all three of the following examples.

A Baskets quilt (fig. 89), dated and signed in the quilting "1931 D.L.," has been attributed to Mary Stoltzfus Lapp. She is said to have made it for her son Daniel Lapp before his marriage to Lydia Smoker in 1934. Another Baskets quilt, dated and signed "1926 M.L.," is also attributed to Mary Stoltzfus Lapp. Yet another was made by Mary's sister Barbara Stoltzfus

Fig. 87
Bars quilt made for Jessie
Bawell (1908-1931) before
his marriage to Rachel Beiler
in 1930, attributed to his
mother Mary Fisher (Mrs.
Daniel) Bawell, eastern
Lancaster County, 1920-25.
Pieced wool top with "Jessie
Bawell" quilted near a corner
and intials "RB" outline
stitched on back edge.
Cotton batting, cotton back,
78" square. *Private collec-
tion. Photograph by Charles
Studio of Photography.*

Fig. 88
Center Square quilt initialed and dated in quilting "GD/1875," one of the earliest dated Lancaster Amish quilts, maker unknown, eastern Lancaster County, 1875. Pieced wool top, cotton batting, and cotton back, 82" x 85". *Private collection.*

Glick. These two women were probably the first to make this particular Baskets pattern in Lancaster County.

The Baskets quilt (fig. 90) was made by Sarah Stoltzfus between 1938 and 1940 for her brother Samuel. Sarah's mother did not quilt but had seen her neighbor Barbara Stoltzfus Glick's quilt and asked Sarah to make five of them. Using cardboard quilt and quilting patterns, Sarah made a quilt for each of her four siblings and kept one for herself.

As expected, the 1931 quilt is pieced with all-wool fabrics, and the quilting is a variation of the feather pattern. The later quilt is less densely quilted and has a rose quilting pattern in the outer border. This practice is more typically found in quilts made in the late 1930s and early 1940s. The materials are wools, but some of them are of a crepe weave, again typical of the later date. Presently fewer than ten of the Baskets quilts are known in the Lancaster Amish community, all made by these three women from the Lapp, Stoltzfus, and Glick families.

Another block design quilt, also rarely seen, is the Fans quilt (fig. 91). It is pieced from wool, cotton, and rayon fabrics. The variety of fabrics, the rainbow array of light colors, and the cotton paisley print back are consistent with Amish quilts made in the 1940s. The central red quadrant of each fan highlights the excitement of this atypical pattern. The blue rayon basket-quilted border is consistent with Amish techniques and acts to unify the quilt. Although unquilted, the blocks are heavily embroidered with decorative stitching alternating in pattern to add interest. The stitching and pattern are reminiscent of silk quilts of the Victorian period. It is likely that the idea for this motif, rarely found in Lancaster Amish quilts, was borrowed by the maker from the English (a term used by the Amish for their non-Amish neighbors).

The Sawtooth Diamond was a pattern shared among the Amish and their neighbors. It seems to have been popular with certain Mennonite and Brethren families in northern Lancaster County (fig. 196) and less common in Amish homes. The Amish version (fig. 92) is pieced from wools, as one would expect. The quilting is also consistent with other Amish quilts made in the 1930s. The red outer border contains the familiar feather quilting, and the triangular fields and center are quilted with plants that bear both tulips and roses. The aqua sawtooth strips are decorated with five-petaled flower, leaf, and stem quilting patterns. The backing, as seen in Figure 93, is made of a bright pink and blue printed cotton fabric. While the tops of Amish quilts rarely contain printed fabrics, there seems to have been no such restriction on what was used on the back. Many backs were also made of fabrics with a woven design. The earlier backings tend to have been of the plainer sort.

When viewing Lancaster Amish quilts as a group, one can see consistencies in patterns and materials with slight changes over time. Also, within the close-knit community there appears to have been some room for adaptation and experimentation, allowing us to see some of the delightful variants illustrated here.

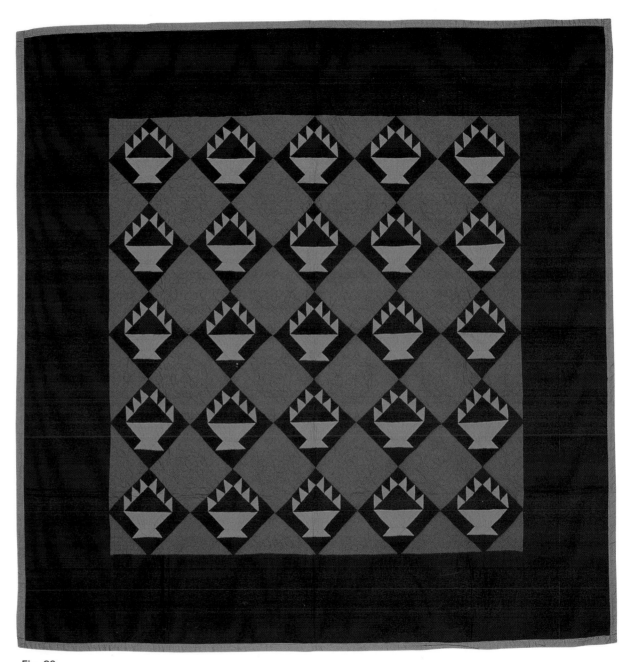

Fig. 89
Baskets quilt, an uncommon pattern in the Lancaster Amish quilting tradition. All known examples were made by three related makers. Signed and dated in quilting, "1931/DL"; made for Daniel S. Lapp (b. 1911), attributed to his mother Mary Stoltzfus (Mrs. Daniel) Lapp (1875-1955), Salisbury Township, 1931. Pieced wool top, cotton batting, cotton back, 80" square. *Collection of Jay and Susen Leary.*

Fig. 90
Baskets quilt, similar to Daniel
Lapp's quilt (fig. 89). The pattern
was chosen by Amanda Smoker,
who did not quilt, for her son
Samuel Stoltzfus. Made by his
sister Sarah Stoltzfus (b. 1923),
Salisbury Township, c. 1939.
Pieced wool top, cotton batting,
cotton back, 80" square. *Heri-*
tage Center of Lancaster County
through the generosity of the
James Hale Steinman Founda-
tion. Photograph by Charles
Studio of Photography.

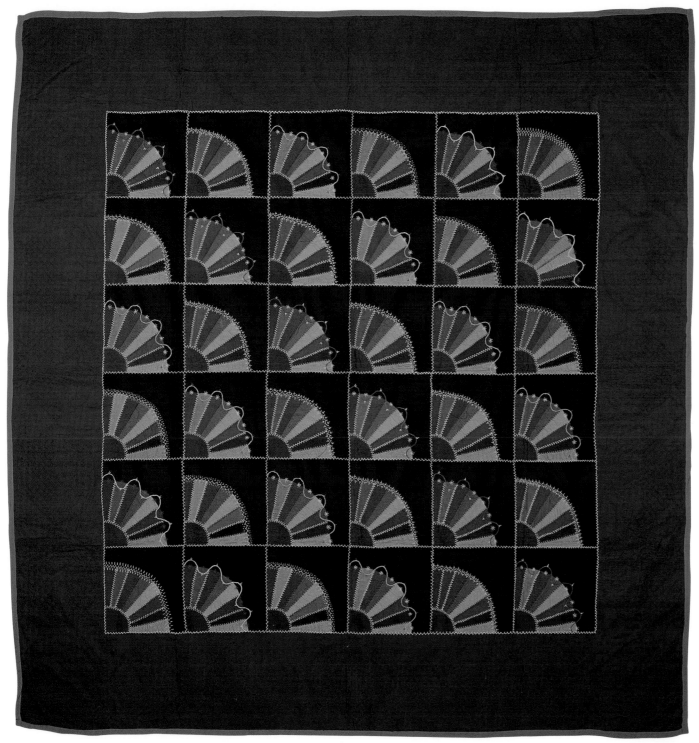

Fig. 91
Fans quilt, a design rarely
made by Amish quilters,
shows characteristics of more
worldly Crazy quilts frequently
made by non-Amish women.
Unknown Amish maker,
eastern Lancaster County,
early 1940s. Pieced cotton,
wool, rayon top with cotton
embroidery stitching, cotton
batting, cotton back, 78" x 81".
*Collection of Dr. and Mrs. Paul
D. Kutish.*

Right:
Fig. 92
Sawtooth Diamond quilt, similar to Center Diamond pattern but a later and less commonly seen pattern. Maker unknown, Earl Township, c. 1935. Pieced wool top, cotton batting, cotton back, 87" square. *Private collection.*

Below:
Fig. 93
Detail of back and binding of Sawtooth Diamond quilt (fig. 92), revealing bright printed cotton material that would never have been used by an Amish woman for her quilt top. The binding is cut wool fabric forming a wide (1 inch) contrasting edge. Pieced wool top, cotton batting, cotton back, 87" square. *Private collection.*

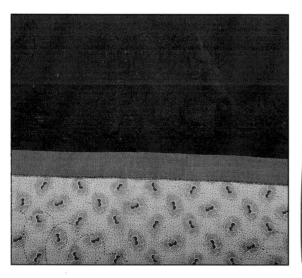

Chapter Seven

TWO MENNONITE GRANDMOTHERS

Although Mennonites maintain close ties among church members, they do not stress the separateness from the community at large that is practiced by the Amish sect. Both religions spring from the same Anabaptist roots established in the 1500s in Switzerland and share some practices such as adult baptism. The fact that Mennonites are more integrated into the community at large precludes specific patterns, colors, or techniques from being associated only with that sect, as happened with the Lancaster Amish community. We are fortunate to have identified two special women quilters, who happen to be Mennonite; they were talented, innovative, and had a strong desire to create special objects for their granchildren.

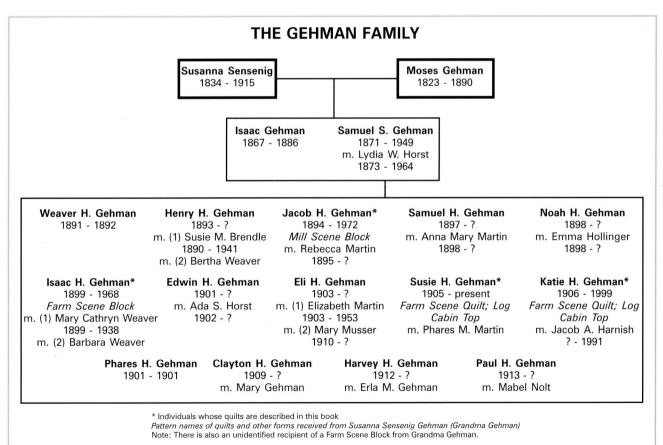

THE GEHMAN FAMILY

Susanna Sensenig
1834 - 1915

Moses Gehman
1823 - 1890

Isaac Gehman
1867 - 1886

Samuel S. Gehman
1871 - 1949
m. Lydia W. Horst
1873 - 1964

Weaver H. Gehman 1891 - 1892	**Henry H. Gehman** 1893 - ? m. (1) Susie M. Brendle 1890 - 1941 m. (2) Bertha Weaver	**Jacob H. Gehman*** 1894 - 1972 *Mill Scene Block* m. Rebecca Martin 1895 - ?	**Samuel H. Gehman** 1897 - ? m. Anna Mary Martin 1898 - ?	**Noah H. Gehman** 1898 - ? m. Emma Hollinger 1898 - ?
Isaac H. Gehman* 1899 - 1968 *Farm Scene Block* m. (1) Mary Cathryn Weaver 1899 - 1938 m. (2) Barbara Weaver	**Edwin H. Gehman** 1901 - ? m. Ada S. Horst 1902 - ?	**Eli H. Gehman** 1903 - ? m. (1) Elizabeth Martin 1903 - 1953 m. (2) Mary Musser 1910 - ?	**Susie H. Gehman*** 1905 - present *Farm Scene Quilt; Log Cabin Top* m. Phares M. Martin	**Katie H. Gehman*** 1906 - 1999 *Farm Scene Quilt; Log Cabin Top* m. Jacob A. Harnish ? - 1991
Phares H. Gehman 1901 - 1901	**Clayton H. Gehman** 1909 - ? m. Mary Gehman	**Harvey H. Gehman** 1912 - ? m. Erla M. Gehman	**Paul H. Gehman** 1913 - ? m. Mabel Nolt	

* Individuals whose quilts are described in this book
Pattern names of quilts and other forms received from Susanna Sensenig Gehman (Grandma Gehman)
Note: There is also an unidentified recipient of a Farm Scene Block from Grandma Gehman.

GRANDMA GEHMAN

The most pictorial quilts made in Lancaster County were probably those produced by Susanna Sensenig Gehman, or "Grandma Gehman," as she was known by members of her family. A variety of pieces created by this gifted woman is illustrated on the following pages, and a genealogical chart of the Gehman family (fig. 94) notes the known recipients of quilts and blocks. Susanna Sensenig Gehman's quilts depict farm and mill scenes. They are buildings and events she viewed every day from her son Samuel's home and included Spring Grove Roller Mill, which he owned and managed in the village of Spring Grove, East Earl Township.

Fig. 94
Genealogical chart showing Susanna and Moses Gehman's descendants and known recipients of quilts and appliqued blocks.

Fig. 95
Farm Scene quilt, cross-stitched initials "Su H G" for first granddaughter, Susie Horst Gehman (b. 1905), of Susanna Gehman. Included are scenes surrounding Susie's home, the Gehman residence, and nearby Spring Grove Roller Mill, owned by Susie's father Samuel S. Gehman. Maker grandmother Susanna Sensenig (Mrs. Moses) Gehman (1834-1915), East Earl Township, 1905-15. Appliqued and pieced cotton top with cross stitching, no quilting or batting, cotton back, 77" square. *Collection of the Lancaster Mennonite Historical Society.*

Fig. 96
Farm Scene quilt, cross stitched initials "K H G" for second granddaughter, Katie Gehman, also a daughter of Samuel S. and Lydia Horst Gehman, by Susanna Sensenig (Mrs. Moses) Gehman (1834-1915), East Earl Township, 1907-15. Appliqued and pieced cotton top with cross stitching, no quilting or batting, cotton back, 78" square. *Collection of The Raymond E. Holland Art Collection. Photography by Bradley A. Schaeffer.*

After her husband Moses died in 1890, Gehman maintained her own house in Spring Grove until poor health necessitated moving in with her son Samuel, his wife Lydia, and their twelve surviving children. Grandson Bishop Clayton H. Gehman, twelfth of a total of fourteen children, recalls this childhood memory of his grandmother:

> Grandma's illness did not destroy her artistic nature. Our house had a second floor porch which extended all the way across the front. A high banister with a closed latticework made it a safe place for older ones and children alike. I spent many days there with Mom and Grandma, watching the activities at the mill and along the creek as well as the farmers in their fields on the south side of the Conestoga Valley. From her place on that sun porch, Grandma painted a picture of the mill with a two-horse wagon loaded with corn standing on the ramp for unloading. A farmer is nearby scooping the corn into the hoist barrel. Grandma made the picture into patches and sewed them on a blanket. That applique work is still a prized possession in our family.[21]

Although no photograph of Grandma Gehman survives, we do have grandson Clayton's description of her in her late seventies: "Grandma was the tallest person in our family, slender, trim, and well-dressed. She was beautiful! When my turn came to ride with her [in the horse-drawn carriage], I soon discovered a warm, cozy, confidence in her presence."[22]

Fig. 97
Log Cabin quilt top, cross stitched initials "K G" for granddaughter Katie Gehman, would be made into crib quilt or part of larger quilt similar to quilt made for granddaughter Susie (fig. 95), Susanna Sensenig (Mrs. Moses) Gehman (1834-1915), East Earl Township, 1907-15. Pieced and appliqued cotton top with cross stitching, no quilting, batting, or back, 37" square. *Collection of Clarke E. Hess.*

A common family tradition is that of a grandmother making a quilt for a grandchild. This has been well-documented, particularly in Mennonite families, in Lancaster County. Emma Snyder, another Mennonite grandmother, made an intricately quilted white quilt (fig. 29) for each granddaughter and a pieced quilt for each grandson.

Like Emma Snyder, Susanna Gehman made special quilts for her granddaughters, Susie and Katie. Some of the grandsons, and possibly other relatives, received single patches or fabric pictures, but her masterpiece Farm Scene quilts were made as special gifts for her granddaughters after they were born in 1905 and 1907. The first of her large scenic quilts (fig. 95) was made for granddaughter Susie Horst Gehman. She was the first daughter of Samuel and Lydia Horst Gehman. On the quilt are eight farm scenes arranged around a large Log Cabin and Star center block. The cross stitched initials "SU. H. G." on the center block identify the recipient as Susie.

The second granddaughter, Katie, received a similar quilt (fig. 96). In this piece the farm scene forms the center of the quilt and, like its mate, it has people and horses displayed around the border. Katie's quilt, however, has a larger, more defined pieced outer border. Susanna also made two small Log Cabin quilt tops, similar to the center of Susie's quilt. Each granddaughter received one in an unfinished state (fig. 97).

Grandma Gehman made a number of small scenes or fabric pictures (figs. 98, 99, and 100). Several other individual scenes also survive that Susanna probably made as gifts, but no other large quilts are known. Susanna Gehman had only two sons, one of whom married and had fourteen children. Of the fourteen, only two were girls. Imagine how busy Grandma Gehman would have been had the ratio been the opposite! Although this group of objects is small, it represents daily Lancaster County Mennonite farm life as interpreted by a superbly talented quiltmaker.

Fig. 98
Appliqued Farm Scene block, chain stitched initials "I H G" for grandson Issac H. Gehman (1899-1968), one of several blocks made as gifts depicting activities seen from Grandma Gehman's porch, where she sat when staying with her son Samuel Gehman's family, Susanna Sensenig (Mrs. Moses) Gehman (1834-1915), East Earl Township, 1907-15. Appliqued cotton top with chain stitching, no batting, cotton back, 13" square. *Collection of Isaac W. Gehman.*

Fig. 99
Appliqued Farm Scene block, label sewn on front stating, "this 12" x 12"
appliqued Patch is/over 100 ys old and was made/by Susanna Gehman."
The unknown recipient would probably recognize this scene as the home
in Spring Grove where Grandma Gehman spent her last few years,
Susanna Sensenig (Mrs. Moses) Gehman (1834-1915), East Earl Town-
ship, 1907-15. Appliqued cotton top, no batting, cotton back, 12" x 12".
Collection of Jim and Nan Tshudy.

Fig. 100
Appliqued Mill Scene, cross-stitched initials and date, "J.H.G 1912," probably for
grandson Jacob H. Gehman (1894-1972), mill pictured would most likely be Spring
Grove Roller Mill, a flour mill along the banks of the Conestoga Creek, owned by
Susanna's son and Jacob's father Samuel Gehman, Susanna Sensenig (Mrs. Moses)
Gehman (1834-1915), East Earl Township, 1907-15. Appliqued cotton top with chain
stitching, no batting, cotton back, frame not original, 24.5" x 24". *Collection of The
Raymond E. Holland Art Collection. Photography by Bradley A. Schaeffer.*

GRANDMA CARPENTER

At about the same time Susanna Gehman was making quilts for her granddaughters, Harriet Miller Carpenter, another Mennonite grandmother living just north of the town of Lititz, was doing the same for her grandchildren. A genealogical chart of Harriet and Uriah Carpenter's family (fig. 101) notes the descendants who received quilts. Present research indicates that Harriet made at least twenty quilts. The locations of nineteen of them are known.[23] Harriet, with the help of her husband Uriah, was undoubtably the most innovative Lancaster County quiltmaker yet known. A page from the Carpenter Bible (fig. 102) reflects their family's history. It records the birth of Uriah in 1825, his marriage in 1853, and the births of Harriet's and Uriah's children: Sumpter, Wayne, and Mary Frances.

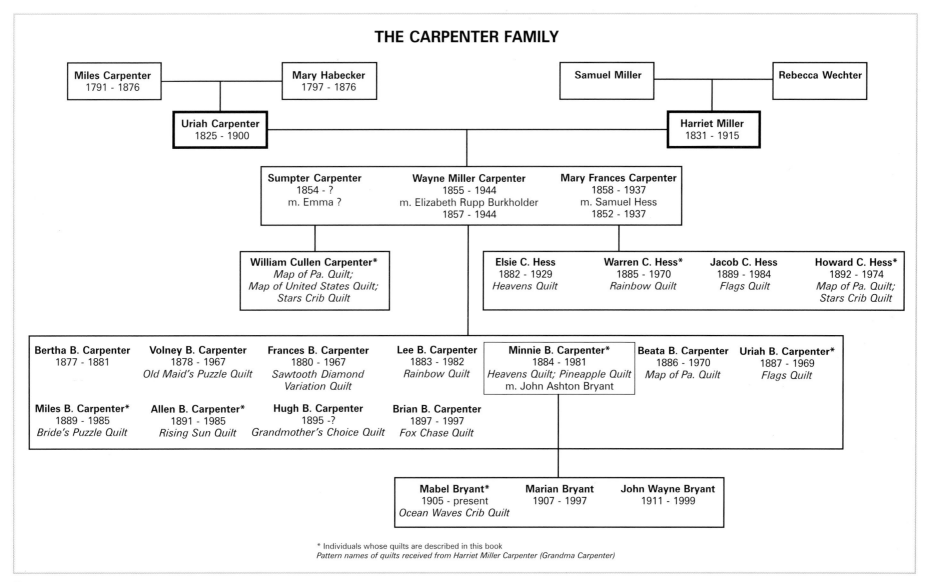

Fig. 101
Genealogical chart showing Uriah and Harriet
Carpenter's descendants and recipients of quilts.

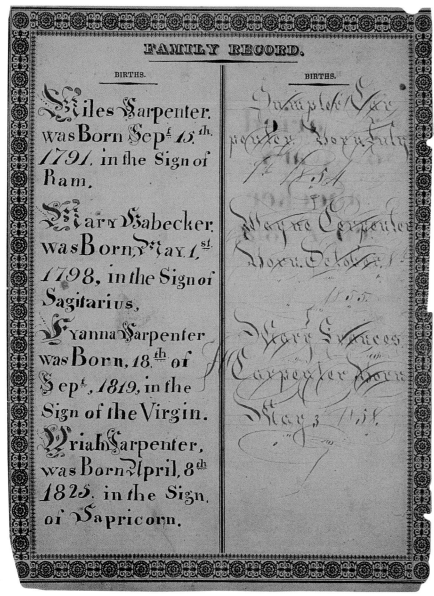

Fig. 102
Family record of the Carpenter family documents Uriah's birth in 1825, his marriage in 1853, and the birth of Uriah and Harriet's children: Sumpter, Wayne, and Mary Frances. Watercolor and ink on paper, probably removed from the Carpenter family Bible, 10" x 7.5". *Private collection.*

Fraktur writing and printed family records were the traditional ways Pennsylvania Germans recorded important family events. Quilts did sometimes serve a purpose similar to the Carpenter's Bible family record. Those made by Grandmas Gehman and Carpenter and the ones illustrated in Chapter Three do more than record. They have the added dimension of being useful everyday objects, presentation pieces with a more personal contact involvement in the receiver's life. By the time Harriet Carpenter's grandchildren were born, fraktur records were out of style in all but Amish households, but grandmothers are still making quilts for their grandchilren in the early 2000s!

A photograph of Harriet (fig. 103) was taken about 1902, two years after Uriah died. Pictured with her, in front of her home in Warwick Township, is her grandson Allen Burkholder Carpenter, for whom she made a Rising Sun crib quilt (fig. 110). Harriet and Uriah had lived and raised their family on a farm called Pine Hill. When they grew older, they built this smaller home on a portion of the land and let the younger generation take over the main house. It is here that Harriet and Uriah made quilts for their grandchildren.

According to family tradition, her Map of Pennsylvania and Map of the United States quilts (fig. 104 and 105) were graphed out by husband Uriah as a teaching aid for grandson William Cullen Carpenter. Harriet then made these designs into full-sized quilts. She documented the Map of Pennsylvania with the embroidered phrase, "Made and presented by grandma Carpenter aged 75" along the lower border of the quilt and added large embellished initials "WCC," for the recipient William Cullen Carpenter, and the date "1906." Lucky grandson William also received a Star pattern crib quilt (fig. 106) from Grandma Carpenter in 1907. Harriet also made two more Map of Pennsylvania quilts for grandchildren Beata Burkholder Carpenter, in 1900, and Howard Carpenter Hess, in 1902. An unmarked Star crib quilt was also made for Howard Carpenter Hess.

Earlier, Carpenter had made another crib quilt (fig. 107), for her first great-granddaughter, Mabel Bryant. Not shy about her age, Harriet stitched "Made and presented to greatgrandchild by grandma Carpenter aged 73 1905." Judging from a surviving example of Harriet's crude signature, she probably did not design the complicated calligraphy used in the lettering of her quilts. Perhaps the patterns were created by husband Uriah or another talented calligrapher living in the Lititz area. Information passed down in the family clearly indicates that Harriet always applied the embroidery herself, but she did allow other friends to take part in the quilting as long as she felt that they were expert quilters.[24]

Most of Harriet's other quilts bear similar signatures addressed to various grandchildren. The use of large decorative embroidered initials, located prominently on the top surface, is seen on a small subgroup of

Sawtooth Diamond pattern quilts (fig. 196) made by other Pennsylvania German women around 1900, in the Hammer Creek area of Warwick and Elizabeth Townships. Harriet also made a Sawtooth Diamond quilt in 1890. It closely resembles the Sawtooth Diamond subgroup and shares some of the same decorative floral stitching patterns that surround the large letters. The lettering on Harriet's quilt reads "Presented in/18-to-90/FBC/Made By/ Grandma Carpenter." The "FBC" stands for her granddaughter, Frances B. Carpenter. This quilt presents more evidence that Harriet was sharing needlework and quilt patterns with neighboring women.

The quilting on Harriet Carpenter's bedcoverings is outstanding. Although the quilting pattern in the central area of her Heavens quilt (fig. 108) is only a simple waffle motif, it is more closely and evenly quilted than most other examples of the period. The border is filled with grapevine and floral patterns executed with the same quilting expertise. As the lettering suggests, it was made for "MBC," granddaughter Minnie Burkholder Carpenter, in 1896.

Another quilt of the Heavens pattern also survives. It stands out as one of the best examples of her quilting technique. Harriet stitched on that quilt, "Made and presented to E C H by grandma Carpenter 1892." No names of heavenly bodies were added. The initials stand for granddaughter Elsie Carpenter Hess, the oldest child of Samuel and Mary Frances Carpenter Hess. Although Elsie lived until the age of forty-seven, she had a mental disability. The quilt survives as a poignant reminder of a grandmother's unconditional love for a special grandchild.

The quilting patterns on Harriet's Rainbow quilts (fig. 109) were more innovative. At the top of the sky in the upper left corner, Harriet quilted the outlines of large fluffy storm clouds. Descending diagonally from them are parallel lines of raindrops ending just above the rainbow in the formation of raindrops. Each stripe of the rainbow is quilted with a different quilting pattern and leaf, floral, and pineapple patterns fill out

Fig. 103
Harriet Carpenter and grandson Allen Burkholder Carpenter, for whom she made a quilt (fig. 110). Photograph taken in front of the home in which she made quilts for her grandchildren, on the family farm, Pine Hill, Warwick Township, c. 1902. *Image courtesy of Edward S. Tochterman, Jr., in memory of Allen B. Carpenter.*

to every edge. The bedcover is truly a masterpiece of concept, color, and execution.

Occasionally Grandma Carpenter even stitched the pattern name of her quilt into her presentation note. The "Rising Sun" was made for grandson Allen Burkolder Carpenter (fig. 110) and the "Bride's Puzzle" (fig. 111) for grandson Miles Burkholder Carpenter. A quilt pattern may have many

Fig. 104
Map of Pennsylvania quilt designed by grandfather Uriah Carpenter (1825-1900) along with Map of United States (fig. 105) as teaching aids for grandson William Cullen Carpenter. Embellished with decorative needle-work along the bottom edge, "Made and presented WCC by grandma Carpenter aged 75 1906," executed by Harriet Carpenter (1831-1915), Warwick Township, 1906. Appliqued and pieced top with cotton outline and other decorative stitches, cotton batting, cotton back, 73" x 84.5". *Collection of Fay C. Garman.*

Fig. 105
Map of United States quilt with states, surrounding lands, and oceans. According to family history it was to be used by grandson William Cullen Carpenter to learn his geography. No presentation statement appears on this example as it does on most of the other Carpenter pieces. Designed by Uriah Carpenter (1825-1900), executed by Harriet Carpenter (1831-1915), Warwick Township, before 1907. Appliqued top, cotton batting, cotton back, 77" x 94.5". *Collection of Fay C. Garman.*

Fig. 106
Star crib quilt, "Made and presented to W.C.C. by grandma aged 76, 1907." Hexagonal plain red blocks set off the Star pattern and are nicely quilted with pinwheel designs. The recipient, William Cullen Carpenter, was seven in 1907. Harriet Carpenter (1831-1915), Warwick Township, 1907. Pieced top with cotton outline and other decorative stitches, cotton batting, cotton back, 51" x 42.5". *Collection of Fay C. Garman.*

Fig. 107
Ocean Waves crib quilt made for another special event. Harriet states on quilt, "Made and presented to greatgrandchild by Grandma Carpenter, aged 73, 1915. The recipient was Mabel Bryant, born in 1905. Harriet Carpenter (1831-1915), Warwick Township, 1915. Pieced top with cotton outline and other decorative stitches, cotton batting, cotton back, 52.75" x 44". *Collection of Mabel B. Joseph.*

names depending on the family or region of the country from which it originates. Finding a quilt name applied by the maker, as part of the quilt, is an unusual occurrence and leaves no doubt as to what name the maker gave to her pattern.

An unusual show of national pride, considering the Mennonite upbringing of the Carpenter family, is exhibited by the Flag quilt (fig. 112) made by Harriet for grandson Uriah Burkholder Carpenter in 1898. It is one of at least two made by Harriet.[25] Her exceptional needlework skills are also showcased in this piece with elaborate floral and fruit quilting, metallic cord embellishments on the top of each flag pole, and each pole stuffed to stand above the surface of the quilt.

Other, almost identical Rainbow pattern quilts were made by at least two other makers. One of the women, Susan Frey Shenk Habecker (fig. 113), was a farm wife living in East Hempfield Township quite a distance west from the Carpenters in Warwick Township. According to the family, Susan made a Rainbow quilt for each of her surviving eight children. Her earliest known quilt is dated 1891 and was made for her second son, Christian S. Habecker, when he was about thirteen years old. See Figure 114. The same date, 1891, appears on Harriet Carpenter's earliest Rainbow pattern, made for "LBC," her grandson Lee Burkholder Carpenter. The inscription on Susan Habecker's quilt, placed between the rainbow and the sun, is done in the same manner as the signatures on several of Harriet Carpenter's quilts, "Made and presented to," with the child's initials elaborately embroidered and the date. The colors used by both women are identical, and the quilts share many of the same quilting patterns.[26] At this time it is not clear which quiltmaker was the original source of the Rainbow pattern.

Susan, who was originally Mennonite and later joined the Church of the Brethren, also produced other quilts for her children. A heavily embroidered Block quilt (fig. 115) was made from white squares joined with red sashing and decorated with needlework. The three centrally located blocks with the initials "ENH" identify the quilt as the property of Ella Nora Habecker, Susan's sixth child, born in 1888. The initials are not nearly as elaborate as those found on the Rainbow quilts. Family tradition suggests that Susan may also have made an embroidered quilt for each child. Even with five other young children, Susan was able to complete this finely stitched quilt by Ella's eleventh year.

The quilting is of the same high quality as that in her Rainbow quilt, but the design reflects the influence of popular culture on this rural Lancaster woman. Red and sometimes blue embroidered scenes on white background quilts were quite the fad near the end of the nineteenth and during the first part of the twentieth century. A number of the Crazy quilts pictured in Chapter Fourteen rely on this type of embroidered decoration. Patterns for use on such quilts were widely available, and many quilts exhibited Kate Greenaway-like figures similar to the ones seen on Susan Habecker's piece. Even rural Pennsylvania was not immune to the mania English author Greenaway created with her late 1800s magazine articles, greeting cards, and books.

Rainbow quilts, possibly by two other makers, are known. One has only the intials "MMB" and the date "1892." It is said by the family to have belonged to Mabel Mae Brubacher, who was born in 1884. The makers were probably Mabel and her mother Emma Witmer Brubacher, Mennonite women who lived in Mount Joy, West Hempfield Township, Lancaster County. Another similar quilt bears the date "1892" and three initials that appear to be "CHZ." There is no history attached to the latter example.[27]

Quilts made by this small group of women are scattered throughout the United States. Fortunately, most are still treasured by family members. Collectors frequently refer to these patterns as Daytime and Nighttime Sky quilts, both of which were made by Harriet Carpenter. The Carpenter and Habecker families know the quilts with the arched rainbow as the Rainbow pattern. Harriet and Uriah's Carpenter's descendants have always called the quilts containing stars and a comet the Heavens quilts. They believe they were designed by grandfather Uriah Carpenter to teach his grandchildren about the evening skies. Although the collecting community has, in the past, attributed all of them to Grandma Carpenter, the Rainbow pattern quilts were created by at least three families of makers: the Carpenters, Habeckers, and Brubachers.

Fig. 108
Heavens quilt, name used by Carpenter family for two quilts Harriet made in this pattern. Needlework lettering, "Made and presented to/MBC/by grandma Carpenter,/1896," indicates it was made for granddaughter Minnie Burkholder Carpenter, who was then twelve years old. Applique work depicts sun, moon, the Milky Way, stars, a comet, and planets, some of which are named and provide even more interest on the midnight blue sky. Harriet Carpenter (1831-1915), Warwick Township, 1896. Appliqued top with cotton outline and other decorative stitches, cotton batting, cotton back, 87" x 83". *Collection of John B. Doughton. Photograph by Charles Studio of Photography.*

Fig. 109
Rainbow quilt "Made and presented WCH by grandma Carpenter./1897," for grandson Warren Carpenter Hess, who would have been twelve years old at the time. Innovative quilting, placed in the dark sky in the form of clouds, rain, and raindrops, is complemented by feather and floral patterns in the rest of the quilt. The Rainbow pattern was also used by at least three other Lancaster County makers. Harriet Carpenter (1831-1915), Warwick Township, 1897. Appliqued and pieced top with cotton outline and other decorative stitches, cotton batting, cotton back, 86" x 95". *Collection of Esther Hess Miller. Photograph by Charles Studio of Photography.*

Fig. 110
Rising Sun quilt with pattern name embroidered along bottom edge with Harriet's presentation comments, "Rising sun. 1901./Made and Presented To ABC by Grandma Carpenter," made for grandson Allen Burkholder Carpenter, who was ten years old at the time. Harriet Carpenter (1831-1915), Warwick Township, 1901. Pieced top with cotton outline and other decorative stitches, cotton batting, cotton back, 75" x 76". *Collection of Harriett Carpenter Faison . Photograph by Charles Studio of Photography.*

Fig. 111
Bride's Puzzle quilt, needlework presentation on bottom border, "Bride's Puzzle/Made and Presented To MBC 1901/By Grandma Carpenter." MBC was Miles Burkholder Carpenter, who was seven years old when she received quilt. Harriet Carpenter (1831-1915), Warwick Township, 1901. Pieced top with cotton outline and other decorative stitches, cotton batting, cotton back, 76" x 74". *Collection of Sarah and Miles (Chip) Carpenter. Photograph by Dennis Griggs.*

Fig. 112
Flag quilt with extraordinary decorative details, besides the usual, "Made and presented UBC grandma Carpenter./1898." Includes date "1777," "Union Forever," eagle with "E Pluribus Unum," metallic cord and stitching, and stuffed-work flag poles all added by Harriet for grandson Uriah Burkholder Carpenter, who received the quilt when he was twelve years old. Harriet Carpenter (1831-1915), Warwick Township, 1898. Appliqued, pieced, and stuffed-work cotton top with cotton outline and other decorative stitches, and metallic cord, cotton batting, cotton back, 88" square. *Collection of Mary Jo Scott. Photograph by Charles Studio of Photography.*

Fig. 113
Susan Frey Shenk Habecker (1852-1924), East Hempfield Township, in a colorized photograph taken when she was a young woman, about the time of her marriage to Christian H. Habecker. Susan was brought up as Mennonite and joined the Church of the Brethren upon marriage. Two quite different quilts (figs. 114 and 115) were made by Susan. *Image courtesy of Dorothy K. Habecker Brubaker.*

Fig. 114
Rainbow quilt, one of possibly eight made by Susan Habecker—one for each of her children. Needlework presentation statement on the quilt, "Made and presented to CSH by mother Habecker/1891," is closely related to work on Harriet Carpenter's quilts. Her earliest Rainbow quilt is dated 1891. The quilting patterns are less intricate than those on the Rainbow quilts made by Harriet Carpenter. CSH stands for Susan's second child, Christian Shenk Habecker, born in 1878. Her first son, Albert, was born in 1877. Was his quilt dated before 1891? Who made the first Rainbow quilt? This one is by Susan Frey Shenk Habecker (1852-1924), East Hempfield Township, 1891. Appliqued and pieced cotton top with cotton outline and other decorative stitches, cotton batting, cotton back, 82" x 88". *Collection of Dorothy K. Habecker Brubaker.*

Fig. 115
Needlework Block quilt made for Ella Nora Habecker (b. 1888), sixth child of Susan Habecker, initialed and dated "ENH and "1897" in central area of quilt. It contrasts markedly with Ella's Rainbow quilt, received from her mother and dated 1898. Needlework figures seen in various blocks resemble Kate Greenaway figures popular at the time. Susan Frey Shenk Habecker (1852-1924), East Hempfield Township. Pieced top with cotton outline and other decorative stitches, cotton batting, cotton back, 82" x 80". *Collection of Dorothy K. Habecker Brubaker.*

Chapter Eight

PAPERCUT QUILTS:

One Technique, Two Interpretations

A quiltmaking technique that is interpreted by two cultures in quite different ways is vividly demonstrated by examining Papercut appliqued quilts made in Lancaster County. The method of creating this type of appliqued pattern on quilts reached its zenith of sophistication at Baltimore in the 1840s.[28] The Baltimore Papercut applique technique and materials, usually red printed cottons on a white cotton ground, soon became popular in the southern end of Lancaster County, near the Chester County, Pennsylvania, and Maryland borders. Farther north in Lancaster County in an area settled by German descendants, Papercut appliqued quilts were reinterpreted at a slightly later date with another palette and type of fabrics.

It has been suggested that the Baltimore quiltmakers were influenced by Scherenschnitte (papercut) presentation pieces made by Pennsylvania Germans as decorative gifts among friends (fig. 116).[29] Although this is possible, it is unlikely that Germanic women in Lancaster County were first to adapt the Scherenschnitte technique to make quilts. The more traditional red and white Papercut quilts of Baltimore and southern Lancaster County predate the northern Lancaster County Germanic examples. It is apparent from the many surviving examples that the use of this method for fabric decoration appeared first in the Baltimore area. Although their patterns were not always as refined, the Pennsylvania Germans were influenced by what the Maryland women were doing with papercut fabrics, rather than developing the technique themselves from the Scherenschnitte presentation pieces being made by their own people.

Nevertheless, Scherenschnitte, the German word for scissor cutting, graphically explains how the process takes place. A design is created by folding paper on itself—as a child might make a snowflake design—decoratively cutting the edges with scissors, unfolding the piece, and using it as a pattern to cut cloth pieces that would then be appliqued upon a ground material.[30] Cardboard templates (fig. 117) made by Jonathan Lowery, a northern Lancaster County resident, for his wife Elizabeth in the early 1900s, would have been designed in this manner.

The earliest Papercut quilt illustrated (fig. 73) is attributed to Lydia Bradley, a Quaker woman of English background from southern Lancaster County. The quilt was assembled between the years 1845 and 1847.

Another (fig. 118) was created by Sarah Jane Mullen. It is dated 1849, with names and dates of relatives and friends who lived in Little Britain Township inscribed in ink in the center of each red cut-out applique. Appliqued blocks alternate with open blocks nicely quilted with a variety of floral, basket, and waffle quilting patterns. One block (fig. 119) is quilted in script identifying the piece as:

The
Property of
Sarah J. Mullen
When this you see
Remember me
When I am in Eternity
October the 19th 1849.

Sarah Jane Mullen was a Presbyterian who later married John Bowman Shaffer, a farmer in Little Britain Township. The quilt is a fine example of the English and Baltimore influence on Lancaster County quiltmaking.

A variation of the red and white Papercut quilt by an unknown maker (fig. 120) uses sashing of a contrasting color. It is also embellished with calligraphic names and small ink drawings and the date 1851. The inscribed locations are small towns such as: Bart, Georgetown, Strasburg, and Mount Pleasant, all located in the southern area of Lancaster

Fig. 116
Scherenschnitte presentation piece made for Elisabeth Wissler (1784-?), Manor Township, attributed to Jacob Botz (working dates 1782-1804). Watercolor and ink on cut laid paper, 7.75" x 6.25". *Collection of Clarke E. Hess.*

County. One signature, that of James Bender, was from Philadelphia. The majority of names, Heidelbaugh, Baughman, Trout, and Pickle, were relatives, neighbors, and members of the Octoraro Presbyterian Church, probably all closely associated with the maker of the quilt. Although the signers were only second- or third-generation German Americans, they were no longer farmers and had mingled with and adapted the life style of their surrounding English neighbors. For the most part they were families of the community businessmen and political leaders.[31]

Another Papercut quilt (fig. 121) from the southern part of the county follows the same formula of red print on white. Unlike the first two Papercut examples, the quilt has neither sashing nor open areas to separate the appliqued blocks from one another. The overall effect is to create a busier, more lively design.

The maker, Margaret Meginness Swisher, was of Irish descent and lived in Colerain Township with her husband Henry, who was a weaver and later a farmer. The Swisher family originally emigrated from Germany to Baltimore in the early 1700s. The signatures in the centers of the papercut blocks are all Swishers or closely related families prominent in business and the Presbyterian Church. It is also interesting to note that several of the men named on this and the two previously described quilts gained high rank in local Masonic Lodges.[32]

Eliza Weidler Rudy's quilt (Fig 122) is a departure from the traditional red and white form of the Papercut quilts. In 1860, about the time she made the quilt, Lizzie (fig. 123) was living with her parents, Samuel and Anna Weidler Rudy, on a farm near the village of Oregon, Manheim Township. Later she later married Isaac B. Keller, who was a minister and farmer.

Lizzie chose as her ground fabric a small-scale printed blue material. Set off by dark green sashing and a pieced sawtooth inner border, her quilt repeats the same appliqued block pattern and fabric. The whole effect, with four hearts in the center of each block, is—in the Pennsylvania German manner—lively and pleasing.

The two orange background Papercut quilts (figs. 124 and 125) are from the Muddy Creek area of East Cocalico Township. The use of bright orange cotton material was common in the more rural farm areas of the northern part of Lancaster and bordering areas of Lebanon and Berks Counties. The orange background fabric immediately sets these quilts apart from their southern Lancaster County counterparts.

Like many of the red and white Papercut quilts, the East Cocalico Township Germanic example (figs. 40 and 124) bears local names and the name and date of the owner "Amanda M. Hyman/March 1863" in the center of the appliqued blocks. They were applied with a fabric stamp similar to a commercially produced stamp previously shown (fig. 41). The owner's name was also cross-stitched on the quilt top. The red fabric from which the appliqued pieces

Fig. 117
Papercut templates created by folding paper on itself and cutting with scissors to desired shape; the pattern could then be transferred to cardboard or some stiffer medium. Part of a group of templates made for Elizabeth Lenhart Lowery by her husband Jonathan Lowery (1852-1926), Warwick Township, 1913-24. Paper, 10.5" square, cardboard, 13" square.
Heritage Center of Lancaster through the generosity of Herma R. Losensky.

were cut is of the same type used in the previously pictured southern Lancaster quilts. Putting it on an orange-yellow ground changes the appearance dramatically, making the piece a statement of Pennsylvania German sensibilities.

A solid-colored Papercut quilt (fig. 125) reflects the same color selection as Amanda Hyman's quilt and is dated "1877" in chain stitch embroidery on the front surface. The Ludwig family, in which the piece was passed down, always called it the Oakleaf quilt. It is believed to have been made by Mary Slaubach before her marriage to William Owens in 1885. The couple were members of the Muddy Creek Reformed Church, now called the Peace United Church of Christ. The quilt was then passed on to their daughter Katie (fig. 126) upon her marriage to Harry Ludwig in about 1930. Katie had many old quilts in her estate when she passed away, and they were always kept in her wedding chest. Upon her death two-thirds of her estate went to her church, and the quilt was kept by Peace United Church of Christ in memory of her.

A Papercut crib quilt (fig. 127) was made by Amanda Bucher Snyder Landis (1872-1976) for her daughter Vera Snyder Landis, born in 1906. Mother and daughter appear together in the Bucher and Snyder quilting party

Right:

Fig. 118

Papercut Friendship quilt belonging to Sarah Jane Mullen, dated 1849, shows influence of English and Baltimore quiltmaking tradition. Sarah, a Presbyterian woman, later married John Bowman Shaffer of Little Britain Township. The centers of the cutout blocks have ink inscriptions of friends and relatives. Centrally located white panel contains a quilted signature (fig. 119). Sarah J. Mullen (1823-1901), Little Britain Township, 1849. Appliqued cotton top with ink inscriptions, cotton batting, cotton back, 113" x 112". *Collection of Sara Shaffer Bush.*

Below:

Fig. 119

Detail of Papercut Friendship quilt (fig. 118) made by Sarah Jane Mullen, showing her white quilted signature square in which is written, "The/ Property of/Sarah J. Mullen/When this you see/ Remember me/When I am in Eternity/October the 19th 1849." Like many quilts made in the mid-1800s, Sarah's bedcover is over 9 feet square. Sarah J. Mullen (1823-1901), Little Britain Township, 1849. Appliqued cotton top with ink inscriptions, cotton batting, cotton back, 113" x 112". *Collection of Sara Shaffer Bush.*

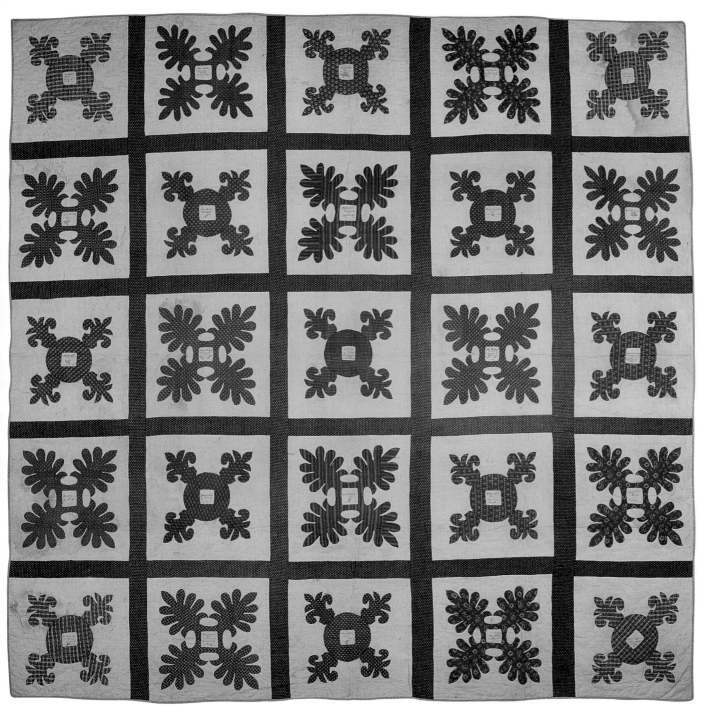

photographs (figs. 216 and 217), taken in 1914. Amanda's family, pictured in that group setting, were Mennonite. When she married Amos N. Landis, a member of the Church of the Brethren denomination, she joined his church.

Amanda copied and adapted her crib quilt pattern from a larger multiple block Papercut bed quilt made by her mother, Fanny Bucher (Mrs. Simon) Snyder. Another quilt (fig. 219) attributed to Fanny Bucher Snyder also has been identified and recorded. The use of a single block Papercut motif is an uncommon occurrence in either Pennsylvania German- or English-influenced quilts and at first glance might be mistaken for a Hawaiian quilt.[33]

It appears from the quilts documented that Lancaster County's Pennsylvania German women made fewer appliqued quilts than the pieced variety. But there is no question that they adapted their quiltmaking skills well to the Papercut design. Using the same technique, two groups of women within one county were able to inject their own sensibilities and create two different but pleasing variations.

Fig. 120
Papercut Friendship quilt inscribed in ink with many signatures of prominent Presbyterian business leaders from small towns in southern Lancaster County. A variety of papercut patterns were combined, using fabrics similar to those in the previous quilt by Sarah Mullen; contrasting color sashing, however, gives the two quilts quite different appearances. Maker unknown, southern Lancaster County, 1851. Appliqued and pieced cotton top with ink inscriptions, cotton batting, cotton back, 92" x 93".
Collection of Cynthia Welsch.

Fig. 121
Papercut Friendship quilt, made up of blocks with slight variations, with names inscribed in ink in block centers of prominent Colerain Township business leaders and Presbyterians closely related to maker Margart Meginness (Mrs. Henry) Swisher (1788-1862), Colerain Township, c. 1850. Appliqued cotton top with ink inscriptions, cotton batting, cotton back, 91" x 90".
Collection of a friend of the Heritage Center of Lancaster County.

Left:
Fig. 122
Papercut quilt made of only nine large blocks, patterned ground typical of fabric choice in Pennsylvania German appliqued quilts. Technique adapted from a style developed earlier in the century in Baltimore, Maryland. Signed in ink "L. W. Rudy" for maker Eliza (Liza) Weidler Rudy (born c. 1840), Manheim Township, c. 1860. Cotton top with inscribed ink name, cotton batting, cotton back, 93" square. *Heritage Center of Lancaster County through the generosity of the James Hale Steinman Foundation.*

Below:
Fig. 123
Liza Weidler Rudy (born c. 1840), photograph taken c. 1875, after her marriage to Isaac B. Keller, minister and farmer. Her quilt (fig. 122) was made before their marriage. *Image courtesy of the Heritage Center of Lancaster County.*

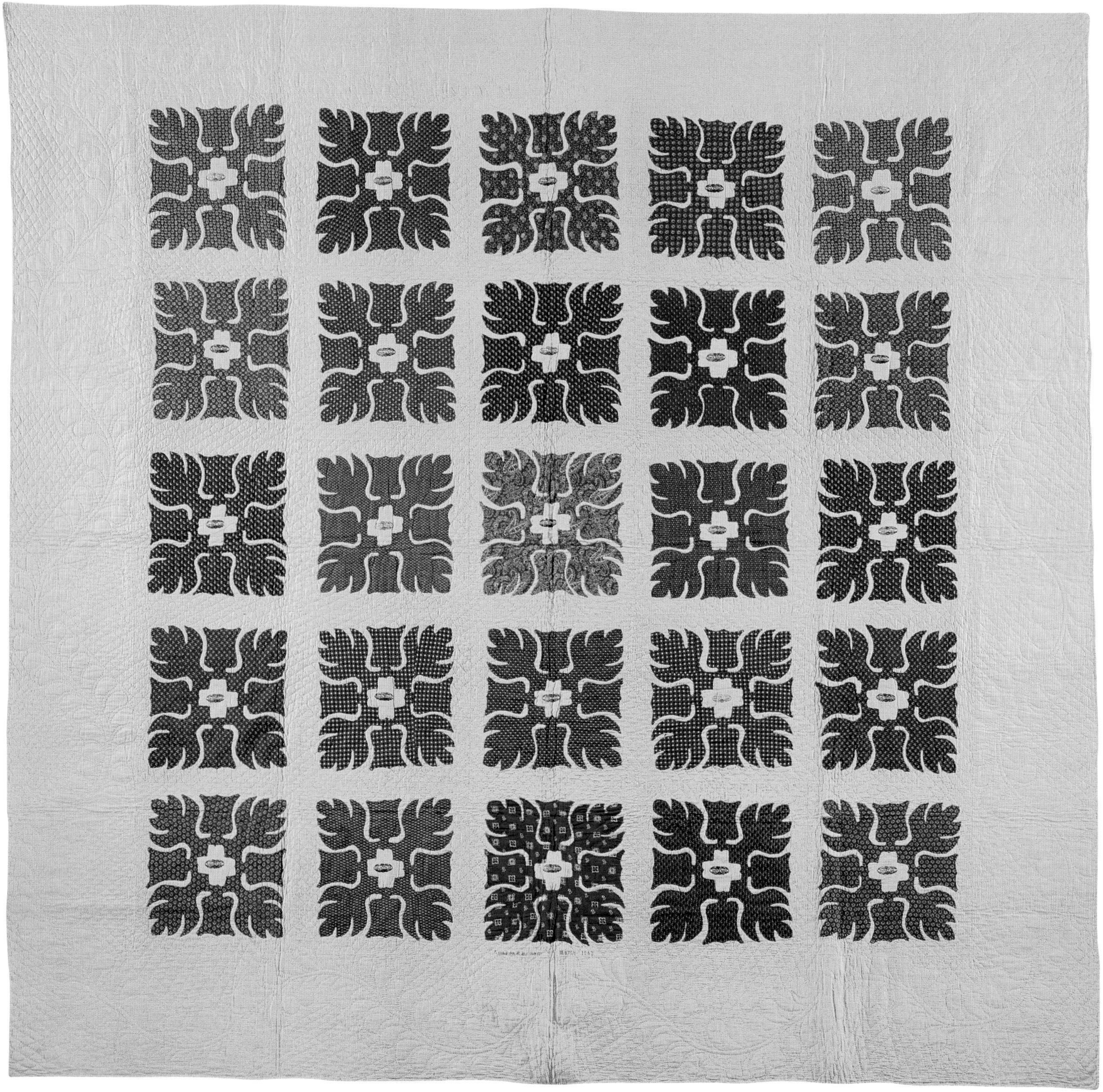

Fig. 124
Papercut Friendship quilt with name of maker "Amanda M. Hyman" and date "1863" cross stitched on quilt. In the center of each appliqued block names of neighbors and friends are stamped in ink, using a fabric stamp similar to one previously illustrated (fig. 41). Each cutout block is the same, but as in previous examples the red appliqued material varies. Background orange-yellow is typically found in northern Lancaster County Pennsylvania German quilts. Amanda M. Hyman (1843-1890), East Cocalico Township, 1863. Appliqued cotton top with stamped ink names and cross stitched name and date, cotton batting, cotton back, 94" x 96". *Private collection.*

Left:
Fig. 125
Papercut quilt made up of two solid-colored fabrics typical of northern Lancaster County Pennsylvania German quilts, chain stitched date "1877" applied to top surface, attributed to Mary Slaubach (Mrs. William) Owens (1855-?), East Cocalico Township, 1877. Appliqued cotton top with chain stitching, cotton batting, cotton back, 90" x 71". *Collection of Peace United Church of Christ.*

Below:
Fig. 126
Photograph, c. 1975, of Katie Owens Ludwig (1898-1985), who received Papercut quilt (fig. 125) to take to her marriage in 1930 from her mother Mary Owens, who probably made it for herself in preparation for her own marriage a generation earlier. *Image courtesy of Peace United Church of Christ.*

Fig. 127
Papercut crib quilt, unusual single-block motif made for Vera Snyder Landis (b. 1906) by her mother, Amanda Bucher Snyder (Mrs. Amos N.) Landis (1872-1956), Clay Township, a member of the Snyder family photographed at a quilting party (figs. 216 and 217), 1906. Cotton top, cotton batting, cotton back, 35.5" square. *Collection of Clarke E. Hess.*

Chapter Nine

THE STARS

Fig. 128 Feathered Touching Stars quilt made from small-scale print fabrics, with color selection typical of northern Lancaster County. Made for Emma Mellinger Burkholder (1866-1924), attributed to her mother Eliza Mentzer (Mrs. Samuel) Mellinger (1834-1890). West Cocalico Township, c. 1880. Pieced cotton top, cotton batting, pieced strip back, 94" x 78". *Collection of John H. and Alice Ann Dinger.*

Star pattern quilts have been identified with all periods of American quiltmaking. Some of the earliest quilts found in Lancaster County feature a large central pieced star surrounded by expensive, imported appliqued chintz materials (fig. 46).

In the latter part of the nineteenth century, with the availability of inexpensive cotton fabrics from the textile mills in New England, southeastern Pennsylvania women had an extensive palette of plain and printed fabrics from which to choose. During this period quiltmakers of the region developed their own interpretation of the star motif. The result is an amazing variety of quilts exhibiting the bold use of color, almost every choice of background color— with white the exception— innovative star forms, a dislike of unadorned space, and a pride of workmanship in fine quilting.

The Feathered Touching Star quilt (fig. 128) was passed down in the Burkholder family of West Cocalico Township in northern Lancaster County. It was probably made for Emma Mellinger Burkholder by her mother Eliza Mentzer (Mrs. Samuel) Burkholder. Emma then married her second cousin, Benjamin B. Burkholder, a farmer, in 1887 at the Reformed Church in the nearby town of Lincoln. This handsewn and quilted example contains all small-print calico materials, with pink used as a startling accent against the major yellow, green, and red color scheme. The combination of pink, yellow, and green calicos is a hallmark of many southeastern Pennsylvania quilts, where a seemingly endless number have been produced. The back of the quilt is made up of alternating strips of contrasting fabric. This is a common method of backing quilts, particularly in the northern parts of Lancaster County and bordering Lebanon and Berks Counties.

Another variation of the Touching Star pattern (fig. 129) was ingeniously constructed of randomly hand-pieced printed cottons. The solid green strips that divide the open squares and form the border pleasantly accent and organize the quilt. One piece of fabric in the quilt (fig. 130) is printed with the centennial celebration dates 1776 and 1876, which helps to date the quilt. The quilt was probably made by Lizzie Metzler and her mother Hettie Shelly Metzler. They were members of a Mennonite family living in Rapho Township near the village of Manheim. Lizzie later married Abram Hernley.

The Metzler women apparently enjoyed making Multiple Star patterned quilts. Another example (fig. 131) showcases their design and quilting talents. Departing from the usual "Dutchy" combinations using yellow or orange, the women made the less common choice of white to contrast with the red and green colored fabrics. The result is a strong visual statement, depending only on the multiple stars and fractional points used as a bordering device. The pattern is set off with simple waffle quilting in which the thread color changes to match the colors of the quilt top. Matching quilting thread to fabric color was a common practice among Lancaster quiltmakers.

A different approach to piecing a Star pattern quilt (fig. 132) was taken by an unknown maker from the Brickerville area in Elizabeth Township. It is pieced from velvets with contrasting decorative stitching outlining each seam. The date "1927" is stitched prominently in the middle of the bottom border. Unlike most Crazy quilts, which this resembles, the whole cover is hand-quilted to conform with the pattern. The choice of contrasting jewel-toned velvets gives it a lush but lively appearance.

A single Star pattern with only a simple border as a frame can make a strong statement. The crib quilt (fig. 133) was created by an unknown Amish woman from the eastern section of the county. Although Lancaster Amish quilts made in the late 1930s began to include rayon blends and cottons, the top and backing of the piece are made up of wool and silk-and-wool blends, suggesting that it was made in the early 1900s. The wreath-patterned quilting between the points of the star and the feather quilting in the border are of the highest quality and typical of Amish quilting. This and the sensitive color shadings offset the simplicity of the pattern and add a sculptural quality to the quilt.

Another example, always known to the family as the Lone Star quilt (fig. 134), has only a narrow sawtooth inner border as a frame. It too has wreath-patterned quilting between the points. The outer border of the piece is quilted with a cable pattern. In this example the piecing was also done by hand and the quality of workmanship is excellent. The family believes it was made by or for Maria Moyer, who lived in Clay Township.

Perhaps the most unusual single Star pattern found (fig. 135) was made by Cathrine Reist Landis. It could be classified as an eight-pointed star but is constructed of pieces arranged in chevrons instead of the usual diamond layout. The sawtooth inner border and strip outer border add unusual accents to this lively quilt.

A label on the back reads, "From Grandmother/Landis to/Simon." This would be Cathrine Reist Landis, wife of Henry L. Landis, who was a farmer in the Landis Valley area of Manheim Township. She also made a Floral appliqued quilt (fig. 166) much earlier in her quiltmaking career. Cathrine probably made this quilt in 1899, when her grandson Simon Landis was born. Just another example of an imaginative Mennonite grandmother creating a special gift for her grandchild.

Frequently Lancaster quilters used small stars and portions of stars to fill open areas around the central star (fig. 136). In this case the maker, Lizzie Heisey Galebach (fig. 137), was not content with just filling the areas with color. Any open yellow background was also quilted with wreath and waffle designs, all of which were surrounded by a three-layer border ending in a bright yellow sawtooth applique.

A note pinned prominently on one corner leaves the instructions, "Mrs. Lizzie Galebach 1919/Please give this quilt to Mrs. Abraham Eshleman/from

Left:
Fig. 129
Touching Stars quilt with randomly pieced stars containing an interesting variety of fabrics (fig. 130). Similar selections of solid orange and brown combined with an array of printed fabrics were frequently used by northern Lancaster County quiltmakers during the late 1800s and early 1900s. Attributed to Mennonite mother and daughter who also made a Multiple Block Broken Star quilt (fig. 131), Hettie Shelly (Mrs. John H.) Metzler (1827-73) and Lizzie Metzler (1862-1938), Rapho Township, c. 1876. Pieced cotton top, cotton batting, cotton back, 84" square. *Private collection.*

Below:
Fig. 130
Detail of Touching Stars quilt (fig. 129), showing an array of patterned and solid fabrics including material marketed for Centennial celebration in 1876. Attributed to Hettie Shelly (Mrs. John H.) Metzler (1827-73) and Lizzie Metzler (1862-1938), Rapho Township, c. 1876. Pieced cotton top, cotton batting, cotton back, 84" square. *Private collection.*

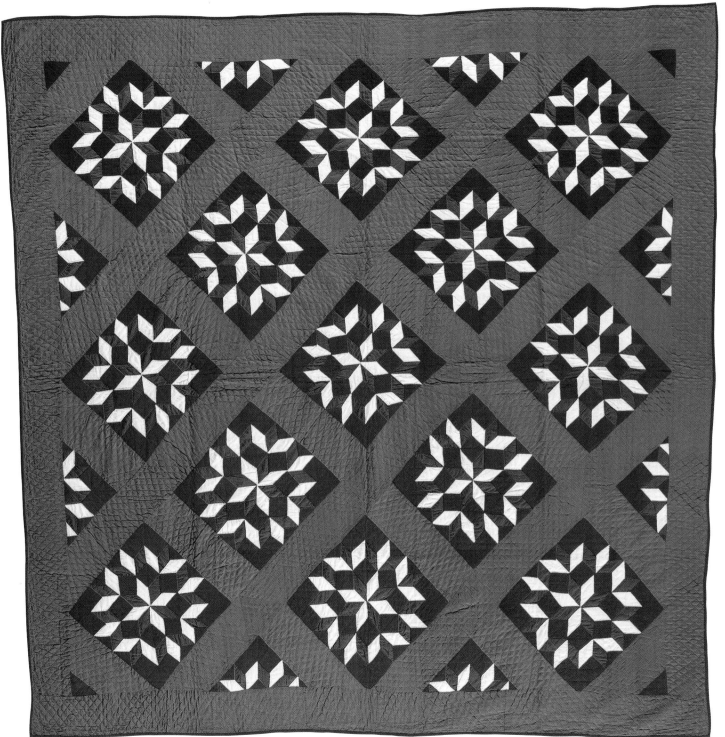

Fig. 131
Multiple-Block Broken Star Quilt made from bold solid-colored fabrics, quilted all in a waffle pattern with threads matching each color, a technique frequently used in Lancaster County quilts, attributed to the same quilters who probably made the Touching Stars quilt (figs. 129 and 130), Hettie Shelly (Mrs. John H.) Metzler (1827-73) and Lizzie Metzler (1862-1938), Rapho Township, c. 1876. Pieced cotton top, cotton batting, cotton back, 92" x 92.5". *Private collection.*

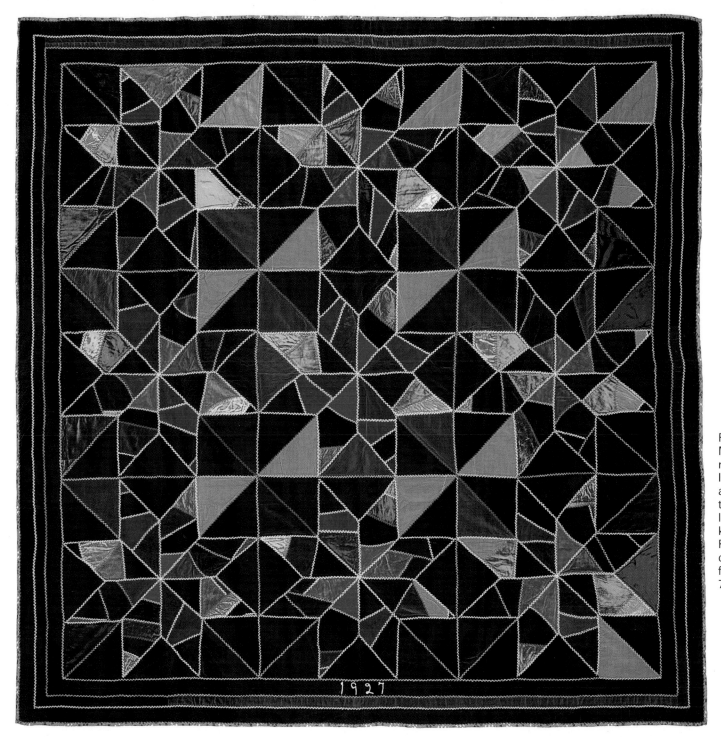

Fig. 132
Multiple Star quilt with random piecing made from lush jewel-toned velvets that are quilted to conform with the pattern, dated 1927 along lower border, maker unknown, Elizabeth Township. Pieced silk velvet top with cotton feather stitching, filling unknown, cotton back, 78" square. *Private collection.*

Fig. 133
Single Star crib quilt is an early example and an unusual pattern for a Lancaster County Amish quilt, maker unknown, Lancaster County, early 1900s. Pieced wool and silk-and-wool blend top, cotton batting, silk-and-wool blend back, 44.25" x 43.5". *Private collection.*

Lizzie Galebach." Lizzie was a Mennonite woman who lived in Mount Joy Township. She probably made the quilt before 1900 and decided to pass it on to her niece F. Alice Eshelman in 1919. Lizzie was the daughter of Samuel S. and Sara Lehman Heisey and married Jacob Galebach, also from the Mount Joy area.

An unknown quiltmaker from Lancaster County created a variation on the same theme using a similar yellow background (fig. 138). Less emphasis was given to the central star, leaving more room for larger multiple-layered corner stars. A simple inner sawtooth border and contrasting edge treatment neatly frame the vibrant piece.

Another rendition (fig. 139) uses the same formula of the large central star surrounded by small stars and segments of stars. An entirely different effect is created when the background is dark green. The quilt is one of a pair made by Katherine Keller Hess that the family has always referred to as Starburst quilts. As in many of the other bold contrasting colored patterns, the quilting thread matches the colors in the top of the quilt. Although not common in other parts of the country, pieced quilts with solid dark backgrounds seem to be found most frequently in the northern sections of Lancaster County and nearby communities in Berks and Lebanon Counties.

It is not surprising that Katherine, a member of the Church of the Brethren, was from a farm near Millway, Ephrata Township, in northern Lancaster County. Born in 1856, she made these quilts about the turn of the century after her marriage to Abraham B. Hess. The couple farmed, and Abraham was also a baker in Ephrata Township. A photograph, taken in the early 1890s (fig. 140), shows the couple with their two children, Harry and Edwin.

A combination pieced Star and appliqued quilt (fig. 141) was made by Rose Wagner Steffy (fig. 142) in about 1898. In so many ways her quilt draws attention to the best attributes found in Lancaster County Germanic quilts. The basic part of the pattern, like the majority of the Germanic quilts from the area, is piecework. The vivid solid colors were carefully laid out so they shimmer from dark to light. Rose dared to mix pinks, oranges, yellows, and reds and place them in contrast with the darker greens and blues. Like the maker of the Star and Princess Feather quilt (fig. 146), Rose added a touch of applique work as an embellishment. Her cleverly placed Papercut heart and bird motifs fill the open spaces within the sawtooth inner border. On each small appliqued bird she placed a French knot to represent an eye.

Rose, unlike many local women, did not do her own quilting; she had it done by the Ladies Aid Society of a church in Lititz. She and her husband Uriah, a stonemason, lived in the small village of Waldeck just north of Lititz in Warwick Township. Many of the quilts documented in Lancaster County were made for family members. Rose made this quilt, which the family called Rising Sun, for her son Thomas.

Bold and beautiful, treasured by family members, valued by museums and collectors, and always exciting to view, the quilts in this category are the stars of Lancaster County quiltmaking.

Fig. 134
Lone Star quilt, so named by
the northern Lancaster County
family in which it descended.
Fine wreath quilting sets off
single star pieced from
exceptionally well-chosen and
crafted solid colors. Attributed
to Maria Moyer (dates un-
known), Clay Township, c.
1875. Pieced cotton top,
cotton batting, pieced strip
cotton back, 85" x 81". *Collection of Carroll M. Rottmund.*

Fig. 135
Single Star quilt with sewn-on label stating, "From Grandmother/Landis to/Simon." Striking pattern and color combinations were created for Simon Landis by his grandmother Cathrine Landis, who also made an appliqued Floral Friendship quilt (fig. 166). Cathrine S. Reist (Mrs. Henry Long) Landis, (1828-1902), Manheim Township, c. 1880. Pieced cotton top, cotton batting, cotton back, 79" x 77.75". *Collection of the Hoover Family.*

Left:
Fig. 136
Star with Small Stars quilt has a paper note pinned on, giving information about the Mennonite maker, "Mrs. Lizzie Galebach 1919/Please give this quilt to Mrs. Abraham Eshelman/from Lizzie Galebach." Likely she made the quilt prior to 1919 but wanted to assure it would be passed on to her friend Mrs. Eshelman. Lizzie Heisey Galebach (1867-1955), Mount Joy Township, c. 1890. Pieced cotton top, cotton batting, cotton back, 82" square. *Collection of Effie Eshelman.*

Below:
Fig. 137
Lizzie Heisey Galebach, maker of the previous quilt, photographed about the time she would have been making the quilt. *Image courtesy of Effie R. Eshelman.*

Fig. 138
Star with Small Stars and Chevrons quilt illustrates an innovative use of various elements of the star motif framed with an inner sawtooth border, maker unknown, northern Lancaster County, c. 1890. Pieced cotton top, cotton batting, cotton back, 82" x 80.5". *Collection of Dr. and Mrs. Paul D. Kutish.*

Left:

Fig. 139
Starburst quilt, one of a pair always known by this name in the family. Dark background and solid-color fabrics add to the boldness of the quilt. Maker was Church of the Brethren woman Katherine Keller (Mrs. Abraham B.) Hess (1856-1929), Ephrata Township, c. 1900. Pieced cotton top, cotton batting, cotton back, 82" x 83". *Collection of Janet A. Fisher.*

Below:

Fig. 140
Photograph taken of Katherine Keller (Mrs. Abraham B.) Hess (1856-1929), maker of the Starburst quilt (fig. 139), with her family. Husband Abraham B. and children Edwin K. and Harry K. appear with Katherine in that order, c. 1881. *Image courtesy of Janet A. Fisher.*

Right:
Fig. 141
Rising Sun quilt combining piecing and applique; maker, Rose Steffy, had quilting done by a local church's Ladies Aid Society. She presented the quilt to her son Thomas as a wedding gift in 1902. Rose Wagner Steffy (?-1926), Warwick Township, c. 1895. Pieced and appliqued cotton top, cotton batting, pieced strip cotton back, 83" square. *Collection of Stephanie Young Kaufhold.*

Below:
Fig. 142
Rose Wagner Steffy (?-1926), maker of the previous Rising Sun quilt. Rose and her husband Uriah, a stonemason, were members of the Lutheran church in the Lititz area. *Image courtesy of Stephanie Young Kaufhold.*

Chapter Ten
PENNSYLVANIA PLUMAGE:
Princess Feather Quilts

Princess Feather pattern quilts are seen throughout the United States, but those made in southeastern Pennsylvania are certainly a flock that stands apart. Identified by their bold colors and innovative design variations, these quilts are a departure from the classic red, green, and blue appliques on white.

Perhaps the most unusual design is the single Princess Feather motif framed within a central diamond (fig. 143). Found in northern Lancaster County, it makes use of the colors commonly seen in that area bordering Lebanon and Berks Counties. The design has elements reminiscent of the Sawtooth Diamond pattern so popular in Lancaster County and the more sedate Center Diamond made by Lancaster Amish women.

Another Princess Feather quilt, this one of more traditional design (fig. 144), makes use of a similar palette of blue-green, orange, and red. It also comes from the northern part of Lancaster County. The maker, Sue Hainly, lived in an area known as Swamp, north of the village of Reinholds. Her quilt is signed and dated "Sue Hainly/1875" with chain stitching on one corner of the inner border (fig. 36). She was twenty-six years old and not yet married to Samuel H. Heinicke when the bedcovering was made. Sue was raised on a farm, and she and Samuel continued to farm after their marriage. They lived in the house that is now the Eichler Art Center in Ephrata, one of the oldest homes in that area. Their two children inherited two almost identical quilts of this pattern, and they remain in the family today.

A darker variation of the Princess Feather design (fig. 145) descended in the Samuel Z. Smoker family of Gap in eastern Lancaster County. The quilt was probably made for Samuel or his wife Barbara Beiler Smoker as youngsters before their marriage in 1913. Smoker is an old Lancaster Amish family name, but by the early twentieth century this particular branch of the family had left the Amish church and become Mennonite. Several other quilts, that are almost identical, have

been found in eastern Lancaster County in Mennonite families with connections to the Amish community. Each one of these quilts had a similar undulating feather border and used solid red cotton fabric against a green ground. Although the Amish rarely made appliqued quilts, they did use dark solid colors like these in their pieced wool quilts.

The Princess Feather motifs become the embellishment in an extraordinary pieced Star pattern quilt (fig. 146). The solid red strips outlining the star and outer border accent the bold design. Most of the other fabrics, including the blue ground, are small-scale printed materials that Pennsylvania German women were so adept at using. The quilt was also made by a Mennonite woman living in eastern Lancaster County. The maker, according to family history, was Amanda Kreider, the daughter of Abraham and Annie Ranck Kreider, who lived in the small village of Farmersville in West Earl Township. Amanda (fig. 147), possibly with the help of her mother, would have made the lively quilt before her marriage in 1853 to Benjamin K. Nolt. Amanda and Ben farmed in the East Earl area and reared six children.

The Princess Feather quilts made in Lancaster County demonstrate the bold use of color, a common practice by Pennsylvania German women of the region. Both solid and patterned fabrics were employed with disregard to the usual red, green, or blue applique on a white ground seen in other parts of the country. Neither is the pattern limited to the traditional four-block motif, as used in the yellow and green background quilts (figs. 144 and 145). Two of the quilts (figs. 143 and 146) exhibit a more innovative handling of the pattern, using it as a central motif and as a surrounding accent. There seems to be no rule governing the direction of the rotation of the pinwheel formation. Some swirl in the same direction, as in the red and green Smoker family quilt (fig. 145), while the others alternate. Although other four-block designs are seen in Lancaster quilts, the Princess Feather pattern appears to have been the most popular.

Fig. 143
Princess Feather quilt,
unusual because of its
single block motif. Added
feathers, multiple
sawtooth borders, and
classic bold northern
Lancaster County colors
combine to create a
unique design. Maker
unknown, northern
Lancaster County, c. 1875.
Appliqued cotton top,
cotton batting, cotton
back, 84" square. *Collection of David P. and Susan
M. Cunningham. Photograph by Jacques Photography, Laramie, Wyoming.*

Fig. 144
Princess Feather quilt of classic four block design, using a palette similar to that of previous quilt. Chain stitched along one border "Sue Hainly/1875" (fig. 36); this quilt is one of pair she made before her marriage to Samuel H. Heinicke. Susan Hainly (1858-1942), West Cocalico Township, 1875. Appliqued cotton stop with cotton chain stitching, cotton batting, cotton back, 90" square. *Collection of G. R. Klinefelter.*

Fig. 145
Princess Feather quilt using four block design and two strong dark colors. Descended in a family of Amish background, from eastern Lancaster County. Made for either Samuel Z. Smoker or Barbara Beiler Smoker before their marriage in 1913, Salisbury Township, early 1900s. Appliqued cotton top, cotton batting, cotton back, 86" x 84" *Private collection.*

Fig. 146
Star quilt with Princess
Feather corner blocks; its
ingenious design of piecing
and applique leaves no empty
space. Bright printed fabrics
accented with solid red
borders add to the visual
excitement of this
bedcovering. Attributed to
Amanda Kreider (1864-1936)
or her mother Annie Ranck
Kreider, West Earl Township,
c. 1870. Pieced and appliqued
top, cotton batting, cotton
back, 86" square. *Collection of
Minnie B. Metzler.*

Fig. 147
Amanda Kreider (Mrs. Benjamin K.) Nolt (1864-1936), (front row, fourth from the left), surrounded by her family, probably taken in the 1920s. She was the owner of, and possibly a maker of, the previous quilt. *Image courtesy of Minnie B. Metzler.*

Chapter Eleven

PLAYING WITH BLOCKS

Fig. 148
Trip around the World quilt purchased from Mennonite quiltmaker by the mother of Kathryn Nissley Strickler (1895-1954) for her hope chest. Note the use and arrangement of seven rainbow colors and compare to Joseph's Coat quilts (figs. 198 and 199). Maker unknown, Rapho Township, c. 1910. Pieced cotton top, cotton batting, cotton back, 85.5" x 84.75". *Collection of Alice Jane Herr Young Walter.*

Single Block Quilts

The seemingly simple task of joining many small equal-sized square blocks together can result in a rainbow of colors and an endless number of patterns. Pennsylvania German quilters were experts in this technique of quiltmaking. Often associated with Mennonite quiltmakers, one of the common variations of single block construction is known as Trip around the World (figs. 148 and 150). It was particularly popular in Lancaster County around the turn of the twentieth century. The pieces were arranged so that the overall pattern appears to be concentric diamonds on point. However, the technique is not limited to Mennonites, nor was it the only type of quilt made by Mennonite quiltmakers. Unlike the Amish, who had more rigid boundaries of community acceptance, Mennonites made a variety of pieced and appliqued quilts that were also borrowed from and shared with the surrounding community. It would be difficult to classify certain patterns, materials, and techniques only as Mennonite.

A classic Trip around the World pattern quilt (fig. 148) was made and put into Kathryn Nissley Strickler's hope chest sometime around 1910. At that time Kathryn lived with her family in Rapho Township. Apparently Kathryn's mother was not a quiltmaker, as she purchased the quilt from a neighboring Mennonite woman. Kathryn (fig. 149) later married Harry Trout Herr.

The top is pieced from solid colors as a wool Amish Sunshine and Shadows would be (fig. 152), but Kathryn's quilt is all cotton. Instead of a broad outer border found in Amish quilts, this border is made up of seven equal strips of the rainbow colors: red, orange, yellow, green, blue, indigo, and violet. With obvious purpose and planning the color progression is repeated from the central block section, where it builds concentric diamonds. Quilting in the outer border is simple, following the pattern; however, each central block is quilted in a teardrop pattern. The exact color combination is used in an entirely different manner in a Joseph's Coat and two Rainbow quilts (figs. 198, 199, and 200). A few other almost identical Trip around the World pattern quilts are known—another Lancaster innovation worthy of note.

Annie Long, the experienced maker who quilted the Fundraiser quilt for Long Memorial United Brethren Church (fig. 68), also enjoyed making Round the World quilts, as her family called them. Annie's quilt (fig. 150) was made around 1915 from scraps she had saved from printed and plain cotton school dress materials. Some of the blocks appear to have been saved from an earlier time, as they date from the nineteenth century. Annie and her husband Franklin B. Long (fig. 151) lived briefly on the Landis farm, which is now Landis Valley Museum. They continued to farm in Manheim Township and were active members of Long Memorial United Brethren Church located in Neffsville.

Fig. 149
Kathryn Nissley Strickler Herr (1895-1954); photographed about 1936 after her marriage to Harry Trout Herr. Her dowry quilt (fig. 148) was made by a neighbor. *Image courtesy of Alice Jane Herr Young Walter.*

Using the patterned dress materials she had handy, Annie carefully laid out the color scheme to create bold contrasting bands of color organized within a bright red border quilted in parallel lines. This was one of apparently many quilts she enjoyed making during the spare time found while raising two children and doing the usual farm wife's chores.

The Amish made, and continue to make, quilts in a Trip around the World pattern; but they call them Sunshine and Shadows (fig. 152) The top layer of the quilt is pieced from solid wool fabrics. As has been noted before when discussing Lancaster Amish quilts, wools and solid colors were used almost exclusively. This example, by an unknown maker, probably dates from the later 1930s. This seems to be the time when Amish quiltmakers embraced the pattern. It then became extremely popular and is still being made today in the Amish

community as a quilt for marriage. The substitution of a meandering floral and leaf pattern for the feather quilting pattern is also appropriate for a later style Amish quilt.

The Amish Sunshine and Shadows rendition has a wide outer border and an inner border with corner blocks consistent with Amish design. Another feature almost always seen in Amish quilts is the total use of black quilting thread. The stitching is fine and even, anchoring the thin cotton batting to the simple blue-grey cotton backing. Most of the Amish versions were made during a slightly later period than the Trip around the World quilts made by their "English" neighbors.

Katherine Salome Hoover Hershey was another prodigious quiltmaker. Like Annie Long; she favored a pattern using single repeated blocks. She made her quilt (fig. 153) in 1917 for her son Willis H. Hershey to take to his marriage. Each of her nine surviving children received one quilt of this pattern for marriage. The family called it the Twenty-five Hundred Patch quilt. The girls were also given extra quilts, but each boy received only one. Willis was the fourth child of the nine children who lived to adulthood. Kate, as she was known, was married to Ephraim Leaman Hershey in 1890. They were a Mennonite couple who farmed in the Gordonville area.

Kate Hershey made quilts for all the family, including her thirty grandchildren, to use on beds and as gifts. The daughters, who were teenagers at the time, remembered helping their mother make the quilts. They estimated that their mother made "upwards of 100 quilts." She made the nine Twenty-five Hundred Patch quilts between 1910 and 1917 from new material purchased especially for that purpose. Kate was criticized at the time for buying new materials for the block quilts. Family comments were, "That's one reason they never got ahead—not economic, did some foolish things."

The Twenty-five Hundred Patch quilt pictured was considered by Kate to be a "dark" quilt, the type she made for the boys. It was based on twenty-five squares to a block with half the squares dark and half light. There were nine different textiles in each block. According to the sisters, they were sewed together on a treadle sewing machine. A photograph (fig. 154), taken shortly before Kate's death in 1950, shows her with her surviving children. Her son Willis, for whom this quilt was made, stands on the far right in the back row. The quiltmaker, Kate, is seated second from the right in the front row.

Another Center Diamond quilt (fig. 155) might be considered a pattern within a pattern. The Center Diamond contains a small representation of the Trip around the World pattern surrounded by broad pink and yellow borders, all set inside a larger "Trip" pattern bordered in red and green. The fabrics in the top are all small-figured prints quilted in a simple diamond pattern. The innovative arrangement resulted in a bold and colorful bedcovering. The back (fig. 156) is made up of larger floral prints, said to be feed sack and shirting materials, laid out in alternating stripes.

Left:
Fig. 150
Round the World quilt (the name the Long family called this pattern), made by experienced quilter Annie Long, who also quilted a Fundraiser quilt (fig. 68). Annie Landis (Mrs. Franklin) Long (1889-1988), Manheim Township, 1915. Pieced cotton top, cotton batting, cotton back, 88.25" x 86.5". *Collection of Ruth A. Myer.*

Below:
Fig. 151
Mr and Mrs. Franklin B. Long, when they were married in 1908. Annie Landis Long (1889-1988) made the Round the World quilt (fig. 150), which was her favorite pattern. *Image courtesy of Ruth A. Myer.*

It was made by a Mennonite woman, Frances Keen Binkley (fig. 157), for her granddaughter Dorothy Ann Groff in 1928. Frances and her husband Zephaniah lived on a farm near Leola. Although Frances designed and pieced one quilt for each grandchild, she did not do her own quilting. As with many families the quilting was a group effort, and she was assisted by her mother Vera Binkley and her four daughters.

Another variation of the single block quilt pattern (fig. 61) was made by Barbara Snyder Stoner for her daughter Ida Snyder Stoner. The Stoner family calls it the Puzzle quilt, but many collectors refer to the pattern as Philadelphia Pavement. Barbara and Ida are included in a photograph taken at the Bucher and Snyder family quilting party (figs. 217 and 218).

As these quilts illustrate, the manipulation of many equal-sized squares can result in a wide variety of patterns and color combinations. There seem to have been few constraints on the way Lancaster County quiltmakers interpreted the technique.

Fig. 152
Sunshine and Shadows quilt, made in the same way as Trip around the World quilts but known to the Amish community by this name. All-wool solid dark fabrics with well-executed quilting, using black thread, make the piece typical of Lancaster Amish quilts made in the 1920s and 1930s. Unknown Amish maker, eastern Lancaster County, c. 1935. Pieced wool top, cotton batting, cotton back, 76" square. *Private collection.*

Left:
Fig. 153
Twenty-five Hundred Patch quilt, known by this name to the Hershey family. One of nine made by Kate Hershey for her children. Son Willis and each other boy received one dark quilt like this; the girls received multiple quilts. Katherine Salome Hoover (Mrs. Ephraim) Hershey (1870-1950), Leacock Township, 1917. Pieced cotton top, cotton batting, cotton back, 79" x 78". *Collection of Katherine Huddle.*

Below:
Fig. 154
Katherine Hershey (1870-1950), maker of Twenty-five Hundred Patch quilt and many others for her children, is pictured here with her surviving children, photograph c. 1948. *Image courtesy of Katherine Huddle.*

Fig. 155
Center Diamond quilt, a pattern within a pattern, made for Dorothy Ann Groff by her grandmother, Frances Keen (Mrs. Zephaniah) Binkley. Frances, another quiltmaking Mennonite grandmother, pieced one for each of her grandchildren but had her daughter Vera Binkley and four granddaughters do the quilting. Frances Keen (Mrs. Zephaniah) Binkley (1862-1935), Upper Leacock Township, 1928. Pieced cotton top, cotton batting, pieced strip back, 80" square. *Private collection.*

Fig. 156
Detail of previous quilt showing pieced strip back made from feed sack material. Frances Binkley (1862-1935), Upper Leacock Township, 1928. Pieced cotton top, cotton batting, pieced strip back, 80" square. *Private collection.*

Fig. 157
Frances Keen (Mrs. Zephaniah) Binkley, maker of Center Diamond quilt (fig. 155), in her conservative Mennonite dress, surrounded by some of her children, taken in the early 1900s. *Image courtesy of private collection.*

ALTERNATE BLOCK QUILTS

Somewhat more limiting is the use of alternating blocks. The following quilts grouped in this category fall under the general pattern name of Irish Chain. The variations reflect the manner in which women of various locations and religious persuasions have interpreted the pattern.

The earliest known version of the Irish Chain pattern is signed and dated "Barbara/Schenken/1814" (fig. 49). For obvious reasons it is usually identified as the Single Irish Chain. The others illustrated are multiple block variations. The most recent version of the pattern illustrated is a Double Irish Chain quilt made during the period 1934-35 (fig. 69).

Most commonly, Irish Chain quilts are pieced quilts containing plain white background fabrics. However, this is not true of the majority of those found in southeastern Pennsylvania. A quilt made by a Quaker woman from the southern part of Lancaster County (fig. 158) comes closest to resembling traditional Irish Chain quilts made in other parts of the country. Its white print background sets off the

Fig. 158
Irish Chain quilt made by a member of the Bradley family, Quakers from southern Lancaster County. With its white background it resembles Irish Chain quilts seen throughout the United States. Exceptional quilting, multiple (five) rows of blocks, and fine sawtooth borders add to the beauty of this well-made quilt. Lydia Bradley (dates unknown), Drumore Township, late 1800s. Pieced cotton top, cotton batting, cotton back, 95" x 93". *Collection of Gloria S. Smith.*

darker prints and solid colors used in the triple chain. The quilting is exceptional, with tight cable and feather stitching in the borders and a pineapple pattern in each white block. Fine inner and outer sawtooth borders add the finishing touch to this classic form. It was made in the late 1800s and descended in the Shoemaker and King families. Family tradition suggests that it was made either by Rebecca or Lydia Bradley, Quaker women who lived in Fulton Township in southern Lancaster County. This is an area settled primarily by English and Scots-Irish families.

The most elaborately embellished Irish Chain quilt (fig. 159) is thought to have been made by Lizzie Kreider (Mrs. Amos) Miller of Manor Township. She was known as a fine quiltmaker and here she showcases not only her expertise with piecing and fine quilting, but also the ability to embellish with applique. What would normally be a common pattern has been made into a bedcovering worthy of special notice. It may have been made for a special occasion, as the date "Mar. 6, 1893" has been chain stitched on one square. Next to the date the penciled letters "A+B+S+M" can be seen. Fine holes where chain stitching has been removed follow the penciled lines. One can only imagine the circumstances that led to the removal of the initials. The busy pattern of

Fig. 159
Irish Chain quilt with appliqued blocks and border, top embroidered in gold silk, "Mar. 6, 1893," evidence of pencil markings and holes where letters "A+B+S+M" were removed. This most elaborate example of an Irish Chain quilt is attributed to Lizzie Kreider (Mrs. Amos) Miller (1864-1937), Manor Township, 1893. Pieced and appliqued top with chain stitching, cotton batting, cotton back, 82" x 80". *Private collection.*

the quilt is enhanced by quilting that not only follows the pieced and appliqued design but also fills the open white spaces with fine feather wreaths and parallel lines. These two white background quilts stand in contrast to the rest of the colored background quilts more frequently associated with Lancaster County Pennsylvania German makers.

A bright and bold version of an Irish Chain pattern (fig. 160) was made by Anne Kreider (Mrs. Jacob) Lefever, a Mennonite woman living in the village of Witmer in eastern Lancaster County. An old newspaper clipping preserved by the family reveals the tragic tale of Anna's death in 1902. The headline tells it all:

PLUNGED TO HER DEATH.
FRIGHTFUL ACCIDENT TO AN
AGED WOMAN.
Mrs. Jacob Lefevre [sic], While Carrying a
Grandchild's High Chair Down Stairs,
Falls Headlong, Breaking Her Neck—Death Instantaneous.

Anne was a caring grandmother, as the article reveals, even during her last days. Her grandchild Phares Lefever was fortunate enough to have received this Irish Chain pattern quilt as a legacy from his grandmother. The contrasting calico

Fig. 160
Irish Chain quilt made by a Mennonite grandmother, Anne Lefever, for grandson Phares Lefever, has three rows of chain and "Dutchy" colors to brighten a room. Anne Kreider (Mrs. Jacob) Lefever (1831-1902), Lampeter Township, late 1800s. Pieced cotton top, cotton batting, cotton back, 79" x 78". *Collection of Evelyn L. Sinner.*

prints are neatly quilted with cable stitching around the borders and a Dresden plate pattern in the open yellow areas. The quilt is another fine example of a Mennonite grandmother's work. While Anne Lefever's quilt plays the dark chain against the light yellow ground, the following quilts (figs. 161 and 162) reverse the pattern colors to use the dark color as the background. Both are made from solid orange, red, and dark green cottons framed with two borders. The first example (fig. 161) is a less common rendition in which the pattern runs parallel to the borders instead of diagonally on point. Note the discrepancy in one of the orange and red twenty-five block units near the border. Did the unknown maker plan this or was it a mistake?

The second example (fig. 162) was made by Amelia Graybill Hosler, a Church of the Brethren woman. She and her husband Israel had a farm in Penn Township in northern Lancaster County. Both Anne Lefever's and Amelia Hosler's quilts appear to have been made in the later 1880s. Amelia's quilting was done all in dark thread, but the quilting thread in the first example changes to blend with the light and dark fabrics. Both quilts are competently but not extravagantly quilted. Another piece, this one by an unknown maker (fig. 161), has a floral device quilted in the open dark squares and parallel curving line patterns in each of the borders. Amelia's quilt (fig. 162) is covered in a simple waffle quilting pattern.

A quite different approach in arranging the blocks results in a quilt having alternating plain and twenty-five block squares (fig. 163). The pleasing arrangement, closely related to the Irish Chain pattern, is made from the common pink, blue, and green prints seen in so many southeastern Pennsylvania quilts. It is neatly laid out with no contrasting borders. Wreath, feather, and cable stitching fill in the large open blue areas to create a unifying effect.

The maker was Ida Louise Witmer Herr (fig. 164), a Mennonite woman living in the village of Strasburg with her husband Frank J. Herr, a farmer and carpenter. She apparently enjoyed quiltmaking. While caring for their six children, house, and farm, Ida made quilts for general household use. She did all her own quilting on a quilting frame she kept set up in the dining room. The quilt shown here was probably made in the early 1900s.

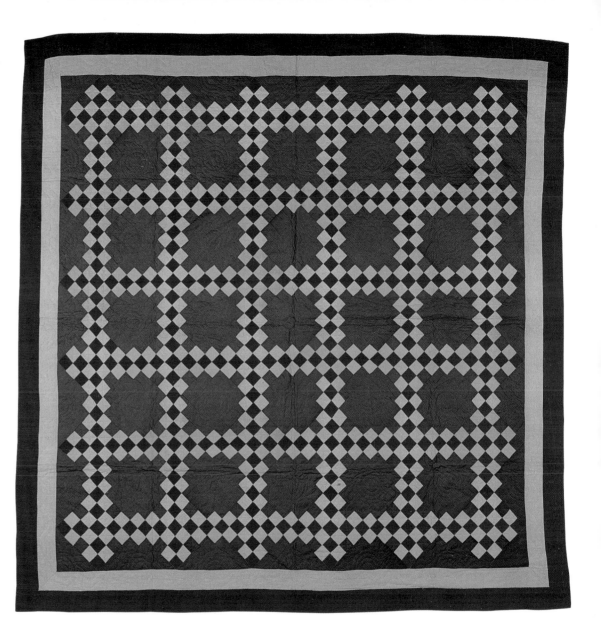

Fig. 161
Irish Chain quilt has color patterns reversed from those of previous examples, with dark fabric as ground highlighted by a triple row of chain. Its layout is unusual because the blocks are set on square instead of point. Note extra red block on one edge. Maker unknown, Lancaster County, late 1800s. Pieced cotton top, cotton batting, cotton back, 82.25" x 81". *Collection of Jay and Susen Leary.*

A matching pair of Irish Chain pillowcases (fig. 206) was also made in the early 1900s by Ann and Rachel Shenk, two unmarried women from Elizabethtown. They are examples of another fabric form constructed in the popular Irish Chain pattern.

The Amish interpretation of the Irish Chain pattern (fig. 165) at first glance resembles other non-Amish quilts of the same pattern. But like most Lancaster Amish quilts it was made from wools of solid colors finely quilted with black thread. Although the Irish Chain pattern was an uncommon choice for a Lancaster Amish quiltmaker, the quilting in the outer border is done in the feather design typical of other 1920s and 1930s Amish quilts. The quilting in the solid blocks in the center of the quilt forms another traditional pattern, a star within a feather wreath. The use of corner blocks in the border is also commonly seen in Amish quilts.

Lydia Petersheim, an Amish farm woman living near Bird in Hand, made the quilt sometime between 1920 and 1925 for her granddaughter Lydia Kauffman.[34] Family recollections are that grandmother and granddaughter went to a dry goods store in New Holland to choose the fabrics.[35] Granddaughter Lydia, who was born in 1914, would have been old enough to take part in the decision-making. The lively combination

Fig. 162
Irish Chain quilt containing the same colors as in the previous piece but laid out on point, a more common arrangement. Amelia Graybill (Mrs. Israel) Hosler (1889-1933), Penn Township, late 1880s. Pieced cotton top, cotton batting, cotton back, 87" square. *Collection of Linda S. Fahnestock .*

Left:
Fig. 163
Alternating Block quilt, a variation of the Irish Chain pattern consisting of twenty-five block squares creating a totally different appearance. Pink, green, and blue calicos used were among the most commonly selected fabrics by Pennsylvania German quilters such as the Mennonite housewife who made this piece. Ida Louise Witmer (Mrs. Frank J.) Herr (1863-1944), Strasburg Township, c. 1900. Pieced cotton top, cotton batting, pieced strip back, 86" x 84". *Collection of Betty Jean Herr Denver.*

Below:
Fig. 164
Ida Herr (1863-1944), the maker of the previous quilt, photograph taken about 1930 after she had reared five children (including a pair of twins). She made family clothes, quilts, and rugs, while working with her husband on the family farm. *Photograph courtesy of Betty Jean Herr Denver.*

of wine, blue, and pink is enhanced by the bright red ribbed polished cotton material the family chose for the backing. As with other Amish quilts, this example was made later than the majority of non-Amish examples of the same pattern. Perhaps Lydia adapted this unconventional pattern from earlier examples made by non-Amish neighbors.

Today the pattern is commonly referred to as Irish Chain by quiltmakers and collectors. It is interesting to note that none of the makers or their families had a pattern name for any of these bedcovers. The nine quilts and the pair of pillowcases illustrated give the viewer an idea of the wide variety of fabrics, colors, and pattern interpretation that was available and used by Lancaster quiltmakers. As with the single block quilts, the Irish Chain variations are graphic examples of the ingenuity of Lancaster County quilters.

Fig. 165
Irish Chain quilt showing Amish interpretation of pattern, using wool fabrics for top, dark quilting thread, and wide borders quilted in a fine undulating feather design, all classic Amish techniques. Made for Lydia Kauffman (b. 1914) by her grandmother Lydia Fisher (Mrs. Christian L.) Petersheim (1866-1954), Leacock Township, early 1920s. Pieced wool top, cotton batting, cotton back, 83" square. *Private collection.*

Chapter Twelve

BOUQUET OF APPLIQUE

When one thinks of the quilting traditions of Lancaster County, the simple geometric forms made by the Amish and the variety of small block patterns created by Mennonite women come to mind. The floral appliqued bedcoverings are not as common [36] and often are thought to have been more English in tradition. When we look at the body of quilts documented during the Quilt Harvest study, we are surprised to find that many of the most intricate and well-executed floral applique quilts were indeed made by Pennsylvania German Mennonite women and not by the English Quaker or Presbyterian quilters. The three floral appliqued quilts discussed here (figs. 166, 169, and 171) were made by Mennonite women living in the northern portion of Lancaster County.

The quilts selected illustrate how women of Germanic heritage adopted the traditional English quilting skills to make the floral bedcoverings that would replace their handwoven coverlets. Mechanization ended the days of men who were professional coverlet weavers and made fabrics affordable to large numbers of women in unlimited choices of color and design.

A Floral Friendship quilt (fig. 166) not only is a well-executed and colorful bouquet of flowers and designs but also is well-documented by the family. A detail from the back (fig. 167) shows two cross stitched panels. The first was apparently worked by the original owner, Cathrine S. Reist Landis, who has inscribed it, "Cathrine Landis/her quilt presented/patches for an/remembrance/dear children/think on me when/this quilt you see/lest i am forgotton/1859." This text was commonly used on samplers and decorated hand towels that were so popular in Pennsylvania German homes in the first half of the nineteenth century.

The next panel of loosely attached muslin carefully documents the path of the quilt's ownership. It passed from Cathrine Landis to her daughter Ella Reist Landis Mumma; to her daughter, Ellen Landis Mumma, who never married; on to Ellen's sister, Ethel Mumma Rohrer; and to Ethel's daughter, the current owner, Kathryn Rohrer Shertzer.

Almost fifty years after working on the Floral Friendship quilt, Cathrine made a pieced Single Star quilt (fig. 135) for her grandson, Simon Landis. Cathrine was the wife of Henry Long Landis, whom she married in 1847. They had fourteen children.[37]

The blocks of the quilt top are further identified in needlework or ink with the names of at least three generations of family and friends. The dates that appear range from 1857 through 1860, the time it must have taken to organize, make, complete, and present the beautifully crafted bedcover to Cathrine Landis. As is common with Pennsylvania German quiltmakers, the plain blocks and background border fabric were made from a small-figured printed fabric. Cathrine added a special finishing touch to the inner border of the quilt by including flat piping of a contrasting fabric within the joining seam (fig. 168). The quilting in the open blocks alternates pinwheels and floral devices, and the border patterns follow the applique pattern. A wide variety of non-repetitive designs was used to create more innovative images than one usually associates with Pennsylvania German applique work. They include pieced work, Papercut technique, and more elaborate floral motifs that contain layered, inset, and reverse applique. Although the occasion of the presentation for Cathrine is unknown, it must have been an important event to warrant the fine workmanship and expressions of individuality each participant put into the project.

Eighteen-year-old Alta Oberholtzer made a quilt for herself (fig. 169) in 1912 in preparation for her life after marriage. Alta was a Mennonite woman living in the Farmersville area of eastern Lancaster County. Her photograph (fig. 170), taken about the time the quilt was made, was done after she joined the Mennonite Church. She is plainly dressed and wears the traditional headcovering of a woman who is a church member. The photograph contrasts sharply with that of her aunt, Anna Mary Oberholtzer (fig. 190). Anna, also a quiltmaker, had her picture taken before joining the church. Anna Mary, with her modish coiffure, chose to wear a draped and beribboned dress adorned with a variety of jewelry. Tragically, Alta Oberholtzer, the maker of this quilt, died from pneumonia two years after she completed it. The unused quilt was passed on to her sister Lizzie Oberholtzer Nolt and then from mother to daughter in the next two generations.

Again, in Alta's quilt, we see the background use of a small-print fabric to set off the bright "Dutchy" orange, red, and green four-block applique. Quilting in the body of the bedcover conforms to the applique with open space filled in with parallel lines. The border is stitched in a cable pattern. This Plain Sect quiltmaker did not spare boldness of color or design while making her quilt.

Right:
Fig. 166
Appliqued Floral Friendship quilt made for, and probably assembled by, Cathrine Landis when she was about thirty-one years old, perhaps for some special occasion. Cathrine also made another quilt (fig. 135) about fifty years later for a grandson. In the interim she and her husband had fourteen children. Cathrine S. Reist (Mrs. Henry Long) Landis (1828-1902), Manheim Township, 1858-60. Appliqued and pieced cotton top with cross and outline stitching and ink names, cotton batting, cotton back, 86" square. *Collection of Kathryn M. Shertzer.*

Below:
Fig. 167
Detail of Appliqued Floral Friendship quilt back with attached cross stitched labels documenting ownership through the Landis family. Cathrine S. Reist (Mrs. Henry Long) Landis (1828-1902), Manheim Township, 1858-60. Appliqued and pieced cotton top with cross and outline stitching and ink names, cotton batting, cotton back, 86" square. *Collection of Kathryn M. Shertzer.*

A more typical Pennsylvania German applique quilt (fig. 171) was made by Anna Hess Franck Erb and her daughter Emma Erb for their niece and cousin Anna Mary Peifer as a Christmas gift in 1917. The family had no specific name for the floral wreath pattern, but fortunately the diary of one of the makers documents her work on the quilt. This Mennonite family lived between Manheim and Lititz in rural Penn Township.

A poignant diary, written by Emma, documents the difficulties and concerns of wartime life in rural Lancaster County. Even though they were Mennonites, who generally adopt a pacifist stance, many friends and relatives were being called to serve in World War I. The whole family took part in War Bond drives, Red Cross sewing circles, knitting scarves for "our boys," and praying for peace and an end to the German aggression. Stores were closed one day a week to save on fuel, and families had flourless days and learned to cook with a flour substitute—even in Lancaster County, a land of abundance.

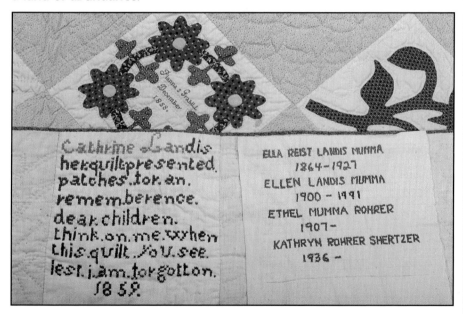

Fig. 168
Detail of Appliqued Floral Friendship quilt showing owner's signed block and decorative piped seam. Cathrine S. Reist (Mrs. Henry Long) Landis (1828-1902), Manheim Township, 1858-60. Appliqued and pieced cotton top with cross and outline stitching and ink names, cotton batting, cotton back, 86" square. *Collection of Kathryn M. Shertzer.*

Amid all this Emma accomplished her usual household and farm chores; was receiving frequent treatments for an unknown ailment; went to a variety of church meetings (Mennonite, Moravian, and other local congregations); and quilted on Anna Mary's quilt. The following excerpts from her 1917 diary document her work:

> Mar 7 Beautiful day. Parents went to John's I finished my black apron and cut patches for Anna Mary's quilt. . . .
>
> June 13...I finished the top of Anna Mary's applicaed [sic] quilt which we started some time in Feb. I think, now for the quilting dear knows when that will be accomplished. Mother wants it for a Christmas present for Anna Mary. . . .
>
> Sept 1 Sat I made a percale dress for Anna Mary.
>
> Sept 2 Sun Anna Mary is nine years old. I saw her at Erbs' Church. . . .
>
> Oct 9 Tues. . . . This afternoon we began quilting on Anna Mary's quilt, we put it in the frame yesterday. . . .
>
> Oct 31 Hallow'een [sic]. . . .We are busy quilting today I quilted A.M.P. in the center not quite half finished. . . .
>
> Nov 8 Quilting on A.M.P. quilt all week could have finished but thought it to [sic] much as I was so tired from working on it.
>
> Nov 20 Tue quilted all day. . . .
>
> Nov 21 Wed Put the last stitches in Anna Mary's quilt this morn at nine.
>
> [A marginal note.] Dec 25. Mother presented Anna Mary with the quilt we worked so hard on.

The initials "A.M.P." mentioned in the diary are quilted in orange thread in an open area near the center of the quilt along with the date "1917" (fig. 172). The rest of the quilting, wreath, floral vine, and parallel lines is done in white thread. As is typical with Pennsylvania German quilts, the background fabric is a small-scale print. The choice of solid red and yellow for the flowers provides a pleasant unity and focus to the quilt.

We are fortunate to have Emma Erb's diary to provide context for a quilt one might otherwise picture being made in an isolated place and time by Mennonite farm women unaffected and unchanged by world problems and the "war to end all wars." Although such information is not available for the two other Mennonite floral applique quilts discussed here, we can assume those makers too were involved in the affairs of their church, their community, and their country.

Right:
Fig. 169
Four Block Floral Appliqued quilt made by eighteen-year-old Alta Oberholtzer for her dowry. The quilt was never used because she died two years later from pneumonia. The essence of Pennsylvania German quiltmaking is exhibited in the use of patterned blue ground fabric and bright orange, red, and green fabric choices for applique. Alta Oberholtzer (1894-1914), West Earl Township, 1912. Appliqued cotton top, cotton batting, cotton back. 89" x 87.75". *Collection of Stella O. Esbenshade.*

Below:
Fig. 170
Alta Oberholtzer (1894-1914), photographed about the time she would have made her Four Block Floral Appliqued quilt (fig. 169). She is dressed in traditional plain Mennonite garb worn by a young woman who has already joined the church. Contrast her apparel with that of Anna Mary Oberholtzer, Alta's aunt (fig. 190). *Image courtesy of Stella O. Esbenshade.*

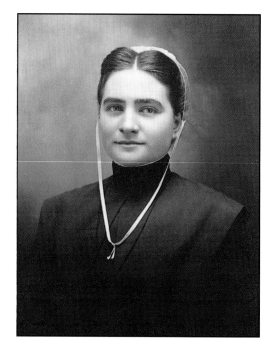

Left:
Fig. 171
Floral Wreath Appliqued quilt also consistent with Pennsylvania German sensibilities, but not as bold as Alta Oberholtzer's quilt (fig. 169). "AMP/1917" quilted in central area. Made in 1917 as Christmas gift from Anna Erb and her daughter Emma to Anna's niece Anna Mary Peifer. Emma kept a diary during the year, chronicling her quiltmaking and the travails of wartime in Lancaster County. Anna Hess Franck (Mrs. Nathaniel Buckwalter) Erb (1862-1946) and Emma Erb (1887-1981), Penn Township, 1917. Appliqued cotton top, cotton batting, cotton back, 87" square. *Collection of Anna Mary Miller and Diane Fisher.*

Below:
Fig. 172
Detail of previous quilt showing quilted name and date "AMP/1817". Anna Hess Franck (Mrs. Nathaniel Buckwalter) Erb (1862-1946) and Emma Erb (1887-1981), Penn Township, 1917. Appliqued cotton top, cotton batting, cotton back, 87" square. *Collection of Anna Mary Miller and Diane Fisher.*

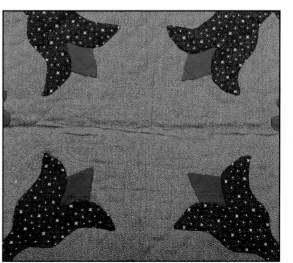

Chapter Thirteen

LOG CABIN QUILTS

The Log Cabin quilt, a pattern familiar to quiltmakers throughout the country, was not ignored by Lancaster needlewomen. Of the examples seen in the Quilt Harvest study, the majority were made by Pennsylvania German women. All but one quilt (fig. 177) shown here came from Germanic households.

Construction is based on building up a block around a square central piece of fabric (fig. 173). The center squares are often of the same material and are frequently red in color. Strips of fabric are sewn to each edge of the side of the central square, then folded, and another slightly longer set of strips is sewn and folded until eventually each block is finished off and pieced to another block of similar construction. The blocks are usually backed without inclusion of a middle layer or batting, as the thickness of the folded strips gives the piece weight and body. Often the backing is merely tacked to the top. If there is any quilting, it is done in the border areas (fig. 180). Of course placement of the colored strips determines the final overall pattern of the quilt. Variations of the Log Cabin pattern are referred to by local quilters and collectors by a variety of names, including Courthouse Steps, Light and Dark, Straight Furrow, Windmill, and Barn Raising. It is interesting to note that, unlike other patterns for which the families frequently had no name, all of the families noted here were familiar with the pattern name Log Cabin and used it to identify their quilts.

The smallest and perhaps the earliest of the examples illustrated is the crib quilt (fig. 174). It is thought to have been made by a member of the Oberholtzer family of Farmersville. This is the same Mennonite family who produced two other quilts (figs. 169 and 188) that were documented in the Heritage Center study.

Except for the center squares and borders, which are of solid hot pink and blue wool, the strips were made from printed wool fabrics. Most of the earlier Log Cabin quilts of this area were made from wool fabrics. By the early 1900s

Fig. 173
Detail of Amish Log Cabin quilt (fig. 180), showing how strips are sewn around the edges of the center orange square and folded, and more strips are added to build a block of appropriate size. This block contains the only two printed fabric pieces in the quilt. Made for Mrs. John Lapp, maker unknown, eastern Lancaster County, late 1890s. Pieced and folded wool top, cotton batting, cotton back, 85" square. *Private collection. Photograph by Donald M. Herr.*

more cotton materials appear to have been used. The layers of the crib quilt are tacked together at each of the pink centers and some additional points. There appears to be a brown and white material placed between the top and backing as a filling. This lively quilt would add color and excitement to any child's bed.

Another optical Log Cabin quilt (fig. 175) was passed down in the Hersh family, who lived in Elizabethtown. Probably made in the 1880s, it contains plain, printed, and woven-patterned wool and cotton materials. They are arranged in what some refer to as a Pineapple pattern. It is a finely crafted example of another striking pattern that can be created with the manipulation of color, pattern, and texture.

A slightly later all-cotton quilt (fig. 176) was made by Sally Echernacht Bicher and her daughter Kate Bicher in about 1897 for the birth of great granddaughter Irma Bucher [Bicher]. Sally was more than seventy years old at the time she worked on the piece. It was quilted with simple parallel lines but has no filling. The top consists of printed cottons with only the center squares of solid red. The Bicker woman were adroit at handling the pattern, creating alternating glimpses of stars and light and dark blocks.

The only non-Germanic quiltmaker represented in the Log Cabin group is Helen F. Ewing Ross (fig. 178) She was a Scots-Irish Presbyterian woman living in Colerain Township in southern Lancaster County. The wife of Winslow Ross, who was a farmer, she was a widow for forty years and supported herself raising turkeys and geese. It is not surprising that her quilt (fig. 177) is filled with goose down. Unlike many, this Log Cabin bedcover, made in the late 1800s, is quilted to conform with the pattern, probably a necessity to hold the goose down in place.

Helen used cotton and wool fabrics, including a variety of printed and woven-patterned materials and a few plain fabrics. Even her center squares were varied. The family remembered her quilting frame being used frequently in the parlor, where she did all her own quilting. Her well-designed quilt, which was one of a pair, is often referred to in the Lancaster area as a Straight Furrow pattern.

Mennonite grandmother Sophia Weaver Taylor made a quilt (fig. 179) for her granddaughter Ida Taylor before her marriage to Milton S. Stoner. Sophia was a Church of the Brethren woman who was married to John Taylor, a stone quarrier, well digger, and butcher. By the time she made this quilt she was in her late eighties. Ida's mother, Catharine Shirk Taylor, had died in 1893 and Sophia made this quilt for Ida and a similar one for another motherless granddaughter when she was ninety-two. When granddaughter Ida grew up she became a prodigious quiltmaker in her own right, having completed more than 100 quilts by the time she stopped quilting at the age of eighty-two.

Sophia's use of cotton materials reflects the slightly later period of her

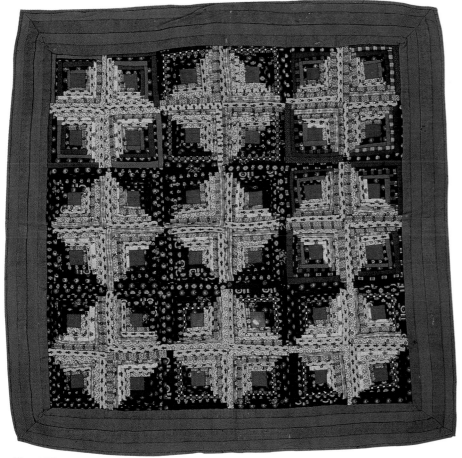

Fig. 174
Log Cabin crib quilt made by a member of the Oberholtzer family, the same Farmersville Mennonite family who produced two other quilts (figs. 169 and 188). Maker unknown, West Earl Township, c. 1875. Pieced and folded wools, no quilting, woven cotton filling, wool back, 38.75" x 37.5". *Collection of Stella O. Esbenshade.*

quilt as compared to the previously described Log Cabin examples. Her choice of solid materials instead of prints for the strips in the central block creates a dramatic focal point. Sophia manipulated her colors well, even splitting the center squares into a light and dark triangle to create a sharper edge on her concentric diamonds. Fabric colors, textures, and patterns are well distributed, giving the viewer a splendid sampling of turn-of-the-century cotton textiles. She quilted the outer borders with parallel quilting lines, changing the color of the quilting thread to match the light and dark borders. Even at a later stage of life, she was still an able quiltmaker.

The quilt that is most easily recognizable as to its origin is, again, the Amish rendition of the pattern (fig. 180). It is an example of what many quilt enthusiasts refer to as a Barn Raising variation. The Log Cabin construction was seldom used by Lancaster Amish women in making quilts and may have been an adaptation picked up from English neighbors at a time when Log Cabin quilts were in vogue. The pattern was more frequently favored by the Amish for use in comforters, pillows, and chair seats, where atypical patterns were often used (fig. 213). This quilt was likely made before 1900 for Mrs. John Lapp by her mother and descended through the family of her granddaughter, Mrs. Ben Stoltzfus of New Holland.

An examination of the familiar feather quilting pattern in the outer border of the quilt helps identify the piece as Amish. The color selection also reflects the Lancaster Amish origin. These quiltmakers favor the use of purples, mauves, pinks, blues, and greens that are not bright primary colors. The maker chose a light orange-red color for her small central squares. Typical of an early Amish quilt, the fabrics—with one small exception—are plain-colored wool fabrics, some having a warp and weft of two different color yarns. The exception may be seen in a light blue printed fabric used in only two logs at the intersection of the central diamond and the border (fig. 173). Since we have no communication from the quiltmaker, we are left with the unanswered question of why this was done. The binding is an early wool fabric somewhat narrower than found in later Amish quilts, and the back is made from a small-scale brown printed cotton material. Although it is not a common pattern for an Amish woman to make, the quiltmaker seems to have mastered the technique to produce a handsome quilt.

Log Cabin construction in the Lancaster area appears to have flourished from the 1880s, with the use of many brightly colored wool materials, through the early 1900s, when cotton fabrics were more commonly used. Each example in the group reflects the individual quiltmaker's approach to creating a quilt limited in pattern by its special construction. The method, in order to be successful, requires the maker to carefully plan, select, and place small pieces of fabric and meticulously sew and fold them. If done in an expert manner, infused with that special sense of design these ladies obviously possessed, the results are stunning.

Fig. 175
Log Cabin quilt using a combination of wool and cotton fabrics artfully arranged in what collectors often call the Windmill pattern. Passed down in the Hersh family of northern Lancaster County. Maker unknown, Mount Joy Township, c. 1885. Pieced and folded wool and cotton top, no quilting, no filling, wool back, 91" square. *Collection of Rebecca Hersh Longenecker.*

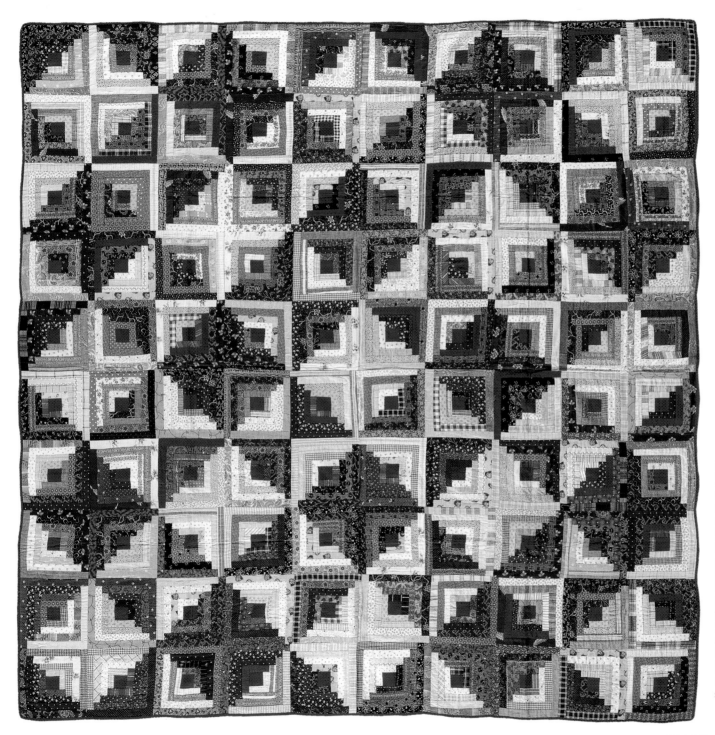

Fig. 176
Log Cabin quilt exhibiting expert manipulation of light and dark segments, alternately visible as stars and blocks. Made by Sally Bicher and her daughter Kate for great-granddaughter Irma Margaret Bucher [Bicher], born in 1897. Sally was more than seventy years old at the time she worked on the quilt. Sally Echternacht Bicher (1823-1915) and Kate Bicher (1849-1939), East Cocalico Township, c.1897. Pieced and folded cotton top, no filling, cotton back, 80" square. *Private collection.*

Right:
Fig. 177
Log Cabin quilt, one of a pair made by Helen Ross, a Scots-Irish Presbyterian woman from southern Lancaster County. This pattern is often referred to as Straight Furrow but was known to her family as Log Cabin. Helen F. (Mrs. Winslow) Ross (1844?-1941), Colerain Township, late 1800s. Pieced and folded wool and cotton top, goose down filling, cotton back, 87" x 86". *Collection of Roy H. Bushong.*

Below:
Fig. 178
Painted photograph of Helen Ross, maker of the previous quilt. Having lost her husband early in life, Helen supported her four children on the family farm raising turkeys and geese. Her quilt is filled with goose down. *Image courtesy of Roy H. Bushong.*

Fig. 179
Log Cabin quilt made for Ida Taylor (1885-1969) by her paternal grandmother Sophia Taylor before Ida's marriage to Milton S. Stoner. Ida's mother, Catherine Shirk Taylor, died in 1893. Sophia made this and a similar one for another motherless granddaughter so they would have quilts to take to marriage. Sophia Weaver (Mrs. John) Taylor (1813-1907), East Earl Township, c. 1900. Pieced and folded cotton top, cotton batting, cotton back, 85" x 84". *Collection of Clarke E. Hess.*

Fig. 180
Log Cabin quilt, descended in Amish family. Fabric in top is all wool and border is quilted with finely stitched undulating feather design, all typical of Amish quiltmaking. Attributed to the mother of Mrs. Daniel Lapp (dates unknown), eastern Lancaster County, c. 1900. Pieced and folded wool top, cotton batting, cotton back, 85" square. *Private collection.*

Chapter Fourteen

PLAIN AND FANCY: CRAZY QUILTS

Fig. 181
Crazy quilt containing portions of neckties, hatbands, wedding gowns, and other family fabrics; blocks on point give some order to the design. Early example from southern Lancaster County by Scots-Irish Presbyterian woman, Veretta Lucinda Neel (1853-1951), Drumore Township, 1885. Pieced silks and silk velvet top with variety of cotton embroidery stitches, tied not quilted, cotton batting, silk back, 66" square. *Collection of Marianna N. Akerman.*

Fig. 182
Veretta (Ettie) Lucinda Neel (1853-1951), maker of the previous Crazy quilt, photographed in 1943 at ninety years of age. Ettie, who never married, kept her quilt stored away in an unused condition. *Photograph courtesy of Marianna N. Akerman.*

Fig. 183
Crazy quilt, whose sixteen block form organizes a busy quilt that
contains fanciful needlework images, comments, and Phi Kappa Sigma
fraternity letters. Red silk border contains maker's initials "ALF" for
Anna Lillie Frantz (1863-1944), Lancaster Borough, 1885-88. Pieced
plain, printed, and velvet silks with a variety of cotton embroidery
stitches and paint, cotton batting, cotton back, 67" square. *Heritage
Center of Lancaster County through the generosity of Mary L. Amidon*

Quilt makers of the late nineteenth century were en-
amored with the concept of the Crazy quilt, and Lancaster
women were no exception. The plain sects—Mennonite
and Amish—and their more worldly neighbors all joined
the Crazy quilt craze. As a result, many examples from
the 1880s through the early 1900s can be found in southeastern Pennsylvania. While other patterns have continued in use over long periods of time, Crazy quilt production appears to have been more of a fad, lasting about
twenty-five years, around the turn of the twentieth century. Other than the Amish piece (fig. 191), the latest Crazy
quilt illustrated is the Fundraiser quilt (fig. 65) made by
the members of Covenant Evangelical United Brethren
Church before 1920.

Although the term quilt is used to describe this textile
category, such items usually were not quilted. More like
comforters, they often were just tacked or tied at intervals
to hold the top and backing layers together. Without the
inner batting and traditional quilting, they probably should
be called covers or spreads. It is likely they were used
more as decorative covers in elegant Victorian parlors and
sitting rooms than as the top layer under which one slept.

An early example of the pattern (fig. 181), dated 1885,
was made by Veretta L. Neel (fig. 182). Veretta, or Ettie as
she was known, lived in Drumore Township in southern
Lancaster County. Like many other residents of that area,
she was of Scots-Irish descent and belonged to the Presbyterian Church. Her parents, Thomas Ross and Verlinda
Stubbs Neel, were farmers.

Ettie, who never married, lived with a sister in later
life. As a result her quilt saw little use. This is fortunate
because, like most Crazy quilts, it is made of silk materials, fancy velvets and ribbons, parts of old wedding gowns,
neckties, and hatbands. With all its delicate fabrics and
fancy embroidery, it would not have survived in this condition had it been heavily used. The arrangement of the
blocks on point gives Ettie's quilt the appearance of constant motion.

Another quilt (fig. 183) contains a variety of velvets,
fancy patterned and embroidered silk fabrics, and a red
silk border similar to Ettie's quilt. The blocks, however,
are placed side by side and not on point as in the previous example. The maker, Anna Lillie Frantz, also embroi-

Fig. 185
Crazy quilt made from fabrics collected by the maker while on several grand tours of Europe with her husband. The only Crazy quilt pictured not having block organization. Central area contains initials "AAG" for maker Alice Anna (Mrs. John S.) Gleim (1840-1923), Abbeville, Lancaster Township, 1887-97. Pieced silk and silk velvet top with a variety of cotton embroidery stitches, no quilting or batting, silk back, 63" x 68". *Collection of Alice Zimmerman Anderman and Nancy S. Zimmerman.*

Fig. 184
Crazy quilt with broad velvet border surrounding heavily embroidered, bold nine block design, signed and dated "ALH 1892" for maker Anna Hoover Landis (born c. 1870), Lititz Borough, 1892. Pieced silk and silk velvet top with variety of cotton embroidery stitches, no quilting or batting, cotton back, 70" x 71". *Collection of Robert L. Janney.*

dered her initials on the outer red border, added paint as a decorative touch to some patches, and accentuated each inner corner with a fan motif.

Other details that set the quilt apart from the previous one are the interesting inscriptions on some of the patches. Several dates appear on the quilt, ranging from 1885 through 1888, suggesting that the quilt was in production for at least four years. One patch bears the initials "HAT" and a drawing of a hat. Another has Greek letters for Phi Kappa Sigma and the initials "RM." The most humorous inscription states, "'And must the weary task/Be done again.'/'A clean shave every day.'/MAS 1885," obviously a man's point of view.

Anna Lillie Frantz was the daughter of Andrew Miller and Esther C. Landis Frantz. A. Lillie, as she was known to the family, never married, so this quilt was passed down in her brother Henry's family. He became a farmer. A. Lillie's sister, Letitia Landis Frantz, became the second woman physician to practice in the city of Lancaster. So it is possible that the inscriptions on the quilt relating to a men's fraternity and the need to shave daily could have come from the family association with a college or university.

The wide, rich red velvet border and large nine-block straight set of the Crazy quilt initialed "ALH" (fig. 184) make a bold statement. Almost every block contains decorative needlework images of flowers and animals. The initials "ALH" in the central square of the quilt have the middle "L" highlighted in red to represent the maker, Anna Hoover Landis. She was the daughter of Isaac and Martha Rhinehart Hoover. The square to the right of the initialed block contains the date "1892." The quilt would have been made after her marriage to John Landis, when they lived in the town of Lititz.

Unlike the preceding examples, Alice Anna Stoner Gleim's quilt (fig. 185) has no internal block organization. The total area within the red silk and brown ruffled border is filled with irregular shaped silk and velvet fabrics organized around a central block containing the maker's initials, "AAG." The decorative elements on the surface range from a pieced house to embroidered silk and metallic thread motifs of a musical staff, ladies, needles, pins, and fabric printed with Kate Greenaway figures.

Alice Gleim (fig. 186), the maker of the quilt, was born in Hummelstown, Dauphin County. Anna was the first of eight children born to Mary Ann Hetrick and Augustus H. Stoner, a Presbyterian couple of Scots-Irish descent. She married John S. Gleim, who established a cigar factory in the City of Lancaster in 1884. The couple lived in an impressive residence called Abbeville (fig. 187), which today survives as a local landmark. As was befitting a wealthy family of the late nineteenth century, the Gleims toured Europe several times. During her travels Alice not only kept a detailed diary but also collected pieces of fabric from each port of call. She completed the quilt between the years 1887 and 1897, using her fabric samples to commemorate her grand European tours.

Right:
Fig. 186
Alice Anna (Mrs. John S.) Gleim (1840–1923), c. 1875, maker of previous quilt. She was well-known for creating fine dresses and quilts. Here she is fashionably dressed for a sitting with a Philadelphia photographer, as would be appropriate for a young woman of means. *Collection of Alice Zimmerman Anderman and Nancy S. Zimmerman.*

Far right:
Fig. 187
Gleim family, c. 1890, owners of Crazy quilt (fig. 185) made by Alice Gleim (fig. 186), on the veranda of Abbeville, their estate in Lancaster Township. *Image courtesy of Alice Zimmerman Anderman and Nancy S. Zimmerman.*

Fig. 188
Wheel and Crazy quilt more
repetitive and controlled than
most Crazy quilts, with
additional needlework on
border that simulates quilting
patterns. Made by Mennonite
woman Anna Mary
Oberholtzer (1876-1962),
West Earl Township, 1892.
Pieced wool, silk, and velvet
top with a variety of cotton
embroidery stitches, no
batting, wool back, 84" x 85".
*Collection of Anna Mary
Charles.*

One hundred years later, on February 25, 1989, the Heritage Center Museum's Quilt Harvest project documented this quilt. That evening the quilt's owner, Alice's great-great granddaughter, took that opportunity to call her father, Alice's great grandson, and tell him about her day at the Quilt Harvest. He had been the one who gathered all the family history in preparation for the documentation. Father and daughter shared the pleasure and excitement of knowing that their family heirloom was appreciated and recorded for posterity. The next morning Alice's great grandson died.

It might be hard to imagine that Plain Sect women—Amish and Mennonites—made fancy Crazy quilts. Two quilts pictured (figs. 188 and 191) were made by just such quilters. The general appearance of the two is somewhat subdued when compared to mainstream Crazy quilts.

Anna Mary Oberholtzer, a Mennonite girl living in the village of Fairmont, West Earl Township, pieced a Crazy quilt and then signed and dated her work on the back (figs. 188 and 189). Anna was the daughter of Lydia Weaver and Christian Hess Oberholtzer, who farmed in this north central area of the county. She made her piece when she was sixteen in preparation for her future marriage and house-keeping .

Anna had her photograph (fig. 190) taken in the 1890s when she was single, before she joined the Mennonite Church. Notice her hair style and the abundance of bracelets, pins, and other jewelry that accent her stylish dress. Compare this with her niece Alta Oberholtzer's style of dress (fig. 170). At the time Alta was photographed she had already joined the Mennonite Church and wore the typical plain dress of a Church member. After marriage Anna would have dressed "plain." She and her spouse, John Landis Landis, settled on a farm near the village of Oregon in Manheim Township.

As mentioned before, the word "quilt" is not entirely accurate. Most examples in this category are held together not with quilting stitches but with knots or tacking at regular intervals. Anna applied outline stitching to the surface of the border of her quilt. It mimics a scroll quilting pattern but does not anchor to the back surface as quilting would do. Her piece also lacks the middle layer or filling associated with the usual quilt. It does have other elements shared by many Crazy quilts: irregular brightly colored silks and velvets, as well as floral and fancy stitched embroidery. The Crazy motif serves as background for rows of half and whole wheel motifs. They are elaborately embellished with embroidery and surrounded by tan circular borders. The same tan material serves as a wide border with its blue scroll quilting. Hardly a plain quilt!

Amish women also occasionally made Crazy quilts (fig. 191). The owner of this example was Susie Stoltzfus, the first of thirteen children born to Lavinia and Amos E. Stoltzfus. Amos had a shoe repair shop in the village of Bird in Hand, Lampeter Township, the center of Amish country in Lancaster County. The quilt, dated 1933 and bearing Susie's initials "SS," was probably made by her mother Lavinia. It was, and still is, traditional in Amish families to prepare several quilts for

Above:
Fig. 189
Back surface of Wheel and Crazy quilt (fig. 188), boldly signed and dated "Anna Mary/Oberholtzer/1892" by maker Anna Mary Oberholtzer (1876-1962), West Earl Township, 1892. Pieced wool, silk, and velvet top with cotton feather and outline stitches, no batting, wool back, 84" x 85". *Collection of Anna Mary Charles.*

Right:
Fig. 190
Anna Mary Oberholtzer, (1876-1962), West Earl Township, maker of previous quilt, wearing stylish dress and jewelry before she joined the Mennonite church and married John Landis Landis, c. 1894. After she became a member of the church her dress would have been of plainer nature and she would have worn a head covering. *Image courtesy of Anna Mary Charles.*

each child well before marriage. In this case Lavinia would have been kept busy making quilts for her ten children who survived infancy. In 1940 Susie married Joseph Glick and they settled in the village of Oregon in Manheim Township to have seven children of their own.[38] No photographs of the Stoltzfus and Glick families exist because of the ban Amish society has placed on making personal images.

This is an unusual pattern for an Amish quilt, but a few similar ones do exist. The Amish also made Crazy pattern comforters that lack the visual structure found in their Crazy quilts. All of the Amish renditions appear to have been made to serve as bedcoverings, and they have extensive quilting. They were made primarily of wool materials, and the Crazy pattern was limited to alternate blocks on point. All solid-colored fabrics were used with decorative stitching but not pictorial needlework. The plain blocks and borders were closely quilted with typical Amish waffle, feather, and floral patterns. The effect is what one might expect in an Amish quilt: the controlled use of a disorganized design carefully held within its boundaries.

Interesting variations of the pattern were made in all parts of the county by women of various religious and economic backgrounds, indicating the wide acceptance of the pattern. Then, as with other fads, production quickly faded. Fortunately, we have been left with a refreshing array of interpretations by the talented quiltmakers of Lancaster County, whose quilts frequently served the purpose of a scrapbook—a gathering place for textile memories.

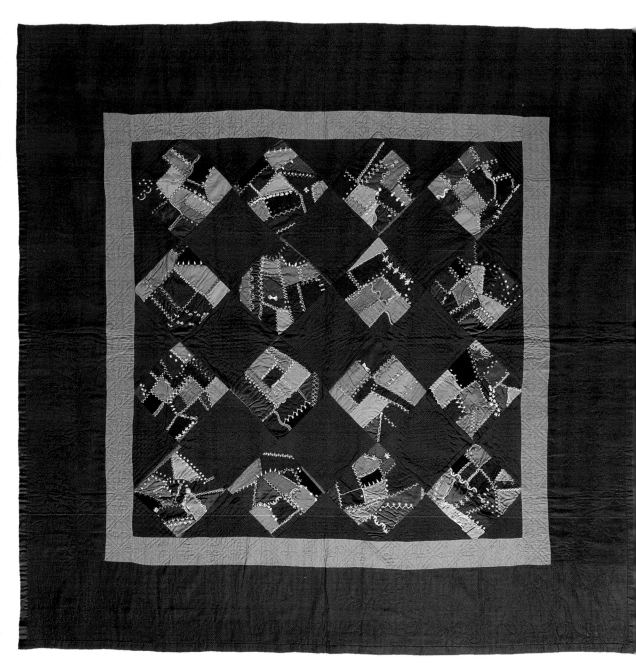

Fig. 191
Crazy quilt with blocks on point separated by plain wreath and waffle quilted blocks resulting in controlled Crazy design. Initials and date "S.S. 1933" for owner Susie Stoltzfus, attributed to her mother Lavinia (Mrs. Amos E.) Stoltzfus, of an Amish family living in Lampeter Township, 1933. Pieced wool, cotton, and rayon top with a variety of cotton embroidery stitches, cotton batting, cotton back, 80" x 78.5". *Private collection.*

Fig. 192
Needlework bedcovering, an unquilted spread created by a member of the conservative Church of the Brethren denomination who worked images from her beloved flower garden onto at least two decorative spreads. Lower right corner block with figure of boy and fish bears the legend, "Made in My 84/year 1925/E. Newswanger," for Elizabeth Clinton Newswanger (1841-1942), Lancaster Borough, 1925. Pieced wool top with variety of cotton embroidery stitches, no quilting or batting, cotton back, 69" x 47". *Collection of Janet Sharon Young Miller.*

Chapter Fifteen

NOT QUITE QUILTS

Like most Crazy quilts, the two textiles pictured (figs. 192 and 194) are not quite quilts. They both have a top surface and back, and the Flag quilt also has cotton batting as an inner layer. Instead of quilting, the layers are anchored at intervals with stitching. Some people refer to such covers as comforts, comforters, or haps, which imply a thick utilitarian cover used primarily for warmth.[39] These examples, however, appear to be more decorative than functional.

One elaborately worked spread (fig. 192) was made by Elizabeth Clinton Newswanger, who documented her work in the lower right corner, underneath the figure of the boy holding a fishing pole and fish. There she records, "Made in My 84/year 1925/E. Newswanger." It may seem out of character that a woman who was a member of the conservative Anabaptist Church of the Brethren would have created such a decorative piece. There are certainly precedents for this apparent conflict of worlds. (See examples of quilts made by Mennonite quiltmakers Harriet Carpenter and Susanna Gehman in Chapter Seven.) A photograph of Elizabeth with her daughter Ella (fig. 193) shows Elizabeth clothed in plain dress. After Elizabeth's death Ella adopted the plain style, too. Both women lived more than 100 years.

Fig. 193
Elizabeth Clinton Newswanger (1841-1942), seated on the left, dressed in plain clothes, maker of the previous needlework bedcovering, photographed in 1941 when she was 100 years old. Her daughter, Ella, is seated on the right. In later years Ella dressed in plain clothes like her mother and also lived to be 100. *Image courtesy of Vivian R. Young.*

Elizabeth made other pieces that also belong to her descendants. One equally elaborate cover bears an inscription saying that it was made in 1923 in her eighty-second year. The maker was born in New Providence in the southern part of the county but in later life lived in the City of Lancaster. Her husband David died early, leaving her with five young children. To support her family she sold candy and did laundry. The flowers on the spreads were designs drawn from flowers in the yard, and she continued to draw and design until her death at 101 years of age in 1942.

A striking Flag quilt (fig. 194) was made by Elizabeth (Lizzie) Bell Linville (fig. 195) in 1920. Her intials "EBL" and the date are embroidered prominently near the central area of the piece. The small flag blocks were one of a variety of fabric inserts that were promotional items packaged with tobacco products. Known as cigarette silks, blankets, and rugs, they were enclosed in small envelopes or wrapped around the package and attached with a strip of paper. They came in a variety of motifs other than flags and were made of silk or cotton flannel with a woven or chromolithographed design. Although men were the major consumers of tobacco, companies marketed these to appeal to women to use in making pillows, covers, quilts, and other craft items. The largest items, like the central flag, were not included in the packaging but were given away as premiums.

This type of marketing was popular from about 1912 to 1915.[40]

Family tradition says that Lizzie's husband Lewis was a streetcar conductor in the city of Lancaster on the line running from the City to Rocky Springs Amusement Park during the years 1900-06. He would pick up the plug tobacco boxes that had been discarded on the floor of the car and bring them home for his wife. One wonders, with all that tobacco being chewed, how enjoyable a trolley car ride really was!

Lizzie pieced the flags together to form the outer areas of the quilt, and she saved a certain number of the small flags to send away to the tobacco company to obtain the premium of the large flag in the center. Lizzie spent a great deal of time outlining each block, each flag, and even the stripes in the American flag with decorative stitching. She appliqued white stars on the blue ground to accent the border and finally completed her project in 1920. Although not quilted in the traditional manner, the top, batting, and back are held together by her decorative chain stitching. Using what were promotional items packaged with tobacco products, Lizzie pieced a bold and patriotic central medallion style bedcover.

Two talented artisans—perhaps we can't call them quiltmakers—created works that reflect their individual talents. Elizabeth Newswanger, not a woman of great means, used plain black materials, and with her design and needlework skills left us images of her beloved flowers. Lizzie Linville, who patiently collected common little giveaway patches, arranged them in such a way as to produce a strong patriotic fabric statement. We are fortunate that family members are cherishing, preserving, and sharing them with us and future generations.

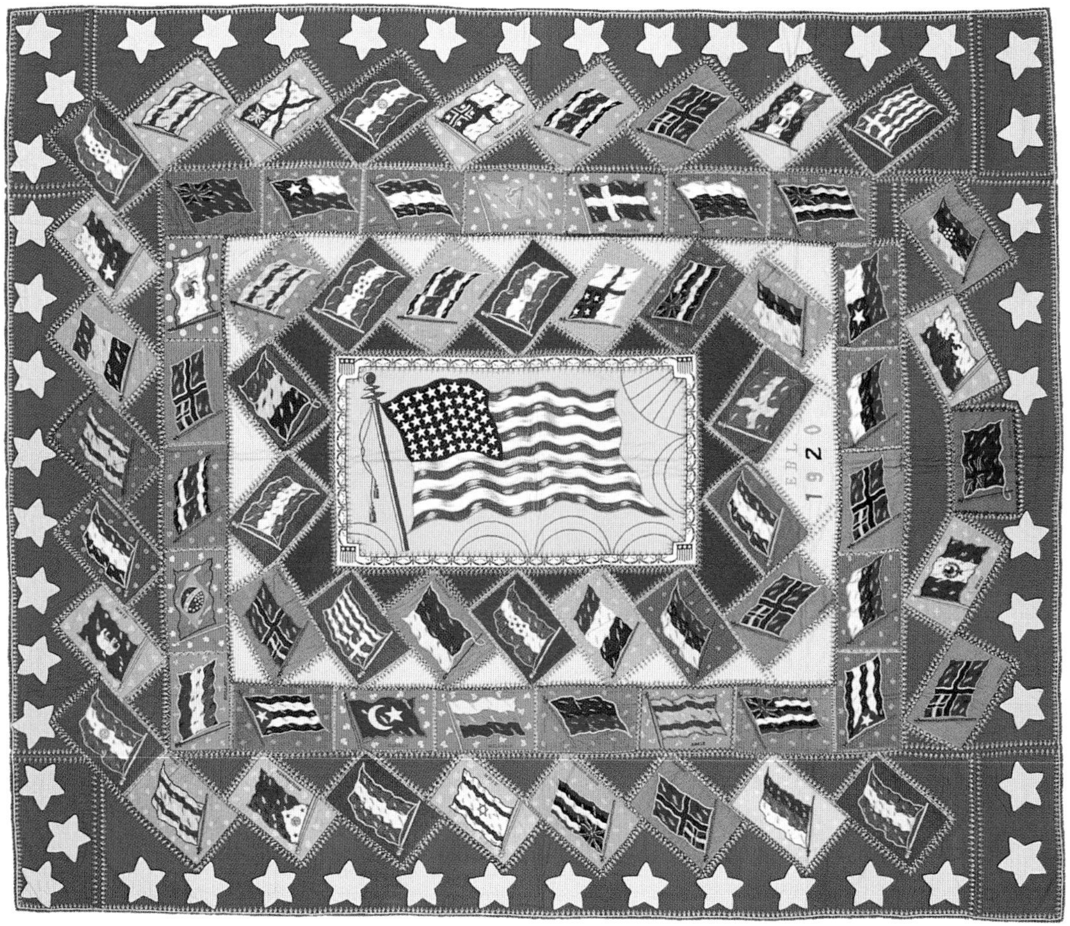

Fig. 194
Flag bedcovering, pieced from tobacco promotional fabrics recovered from trolley car refuse. Dated and initialed on front "EBL/1920, " for maker Lizzie Bell Linville, whose husband, Lewis Linville, was a streetcar conductor. Maker Lizzie Bell Linville (1873-1953), Borough of Lancaster, 1920. Pieced cotton and cotton flannel top with a variety of cotton embroidery stitches, no quilting, cotton batting, cotton back, 65" x 80". *Collection of Alma F. Clendenin.*

Fig. 195
Lizzie Bell Linville (1873-1953), first person in upper row on the left, photographed at a family picnic in 1936. Lizzie was the maker of the Flag bedcovering (fig. 194). *Image courtesy of Alma F. Clendenin.*

Chapter Sixteen

ONLY IN LANCASTER COUNTY

By design, color, and innovation, some quilts can be immediately identified as being made in Lancaster County. Most are associated with Mennonite and Church of the Brethren women. The Mennonites were part of the Anabaptist movement that arose in Europe in the early 1500s, while the Church of the Brethren had its roots in Pietism and sprang up independently of other Anabaptists in the early 1700s. Both groups, like the Amish, follow the practice of adult baptism. Church of the Brethren members employ total immersion rather than the sprinkling of water in the practice of baptism. Neither group maintained the separateness from the larger Pennsylvania German community that is seen among the Amish today. Therefore, their sharing of quilt patterns, colors, techniques, and inclusion in quilting groups would more likely have been extended to neighboring women.

The pattern of the bold Sawtooth Diamond quilt (fig. 196) is found in other parts of the country and was occasionally made by Lancaster Amish women. But those quilts adorned with large embroidered initials in the central area of the diamond seem to have been made only by a small group of Pennsylvania German women living in the Hammer Creek area of Warwick and Elizabeth Townships. It is likely that patterns for the embroidery on these quilts were shared among neighboring women, as identical embroidered embellishments appear on quilts by various makers, including Harriet Carpenter. The quilts were usually made from contrasting solid-colored fabrics of colors associated with Pennsylvania German quiltmaking: green and

red, yellow and maroon, orange and red, and some even less likely combinations.

The initials in the center, "ARB," identify the owner as Ada R. Brubaker (fig. 38). She was a Mennonite who lived on Brubaker Valley Road near the Hammer Creek in Elizabeth Township before her marriage to Benjamin K. Miller. The quilt was probably made for her when she was a girl by her mother Lizzie Risser Brubaker, the wife of Peter Hess Brubaker. Note the similarity to needlework Harriet Carpenter used on her grandchildren's quilts featured in Chapter Seven.

In comparing this Sawtooth Diamond example to its counterpart Amish quilt (fig. 92), one finds differences other than the prominent initials. Close examination reveals that Ada's is all cotton and the Amish example is pieced from wools. Until the introduction of synthetic blends, wools were the material of choice for use by Lancaster Amish women in their quilt tops. Although local Amish women used waffle and wreath quilting designs, as appear in Ada's quilt, the cable stitching in the outer border would be an unusual choice for a Lancaster Amish quilter. More often the Amish quilts have feather quilting in the outer borders.

A classic pattern, which does not require close inspection to be identified as a Lancaster County quilt, is the Star Variation of the Postage Stamp pattern (fig. 197). It was made almost exclusively by women living in and near the town of Bowmansville in Brecknock Township. It is so closely identified with the area that dealers and collectors often refer to it as

Fig. 196
Sawtooth Diamond quilt with embroidered initials, a pattern made by women living in the Hammer Creek area north of the town of Lititz; the needlework is similar to that done by quiltmakers Harriet Carpenter and Susan Habecker, whose work is discussed in Chapter Seven. Large embroidered initials "ARB" identify owner Ada R. Brubaker (1882-?), attributed to Ada's mother Lizzie Risser (Mrs. Peter Hess) Brubaker (1861-?), Elizabeth Township, c. 1900. Pieced cotton top with cotton outline stitched initials, cotton batting, cotton back, 76" square. *Private collection.*

Fig. 197
Single Block Star quilt known to collectors as Bowmansville Star pattern because it is found most frequently in Mennonite homes near the town of Bowmansville, northeastern Lancaster County. Block size is usually 1-½" square, and the arrangement of dark and light patterns varies little from quilt to quilt. Maker unknown, Brecknock Township, c. 1900. Pieced cotton top, cotton batting, cotton back, 88" square. *Private collection.*

the Bowmansville Star. Although the maker of this example is unknown, it was purchased from a family living in that town. The pattern is usually associated with Mennonite families, as this group made up the majority of farm families living in that rural Brecknock Township area in the early 1900s when these quilts were being made.

Typical examples of the pattern are made up of pieces no larger than 1½ inches square and have a similarity of distribution of light and dark squares that is almost formulaic. The majority of fabrics are printed dress cottons with an occasional line of solid squares for accent. The most successful designers used contrasting dark and light combinations in a zigzag arrangement to accent the inner corners and borders. It required talent, persistence, and an eye for good design for a quiltmaker to create such a bold and vivid statement. Although the work demands careful and close attention to detail, the impact is best appreciated from afar.

Just as strongly identified with rural northeastern Lancaster County is the Joseph's Coat pattern quilt (figs. 198 and 199). A small quilt (fig. 200), related to the second large quilt, also survives. Sometimes they are called Rainbow quilts, but most collectors refer to this particular pattern arrangement as Joseph's Coat, if the colors in the main field are repeated as slanting borders.

The first quilt (fig. 198) was purchased from the estate of Ivan Hershey Snyder and belonged to his parents Phares and Anna Hershey Snyder, who lived in the Lititz area. It probably was made around 1900. The colors are the traditional rainbow hues memorized by all school children: red, orange, yellow, green, blue, indigo, and violet. Although the Snyder piece is an unusually vivid color survival, this exact formula is repeated in most of the known examples. The manner of quilting is also common to many of the other Joseph's Coat quilts. Each colored strip in the central area has its own quilting pattern. In the example shown here, all of the red strips are quilted with a Greek key pattern, orange with parallel undulating lines, yellow with waffle quilting, and so on. The border is quilted in a cable pattern.

The makers of the second large Rainbow quilt (fig. 199) chose to stitch the bedcovering using only waffle pattern quilting in the center field and cable stitching in the border. Note that the same color arrangement was used in both quilts. This quilt belonged to Amanda Myer and may have been made by both Amanda and her mother Leah Rife Myer. The Myers were members of the Church of the Brethren and lived in the New Holland area. Amanda married Henry Metzler, a Mennonite, and they settled in the New Holland-Farmersville area.

There was at least one other large quilt of this pattern made in the Myer family, which referred to such pieces as their Rainbow quilts. Amanda also owned a crib quilt (fig. 200). According to the family, it was made from scraps left over from the larger quilts. It was put together in a haphazard but delightful way, and no fabric was wasted. Rows of semi-circular quilting seem to have been placed with no particular regard to the pattern. This too adds to its charm. It obviously received heavy use by the family, and the original bright colors have faded over the years.

In the late 1800s and early 1900s, quilting traditions were strong among the Pennsylvania German women in Lancaster County. In documenting the quilts chosen for this chapter (Sawtooth Diamond, Postage Stamp, and Rainbow or Jacob's Coat patterns) it was found that almost identical quilts were being made by neighbors belonging to both sects. It is not surprising that in the northeastern section of the county, where large populations of these two congregations lived, intermarriage and the transfer of quilt patterns and techniques went hand in hand. The resulting quilts give Lancaster County residents a reason to be proud of their quilting traditions.

Fig. 198
Joseph's Coat quilt pieced from rainbow-colored strips of fabric, each having its own quilting pattern. Compare the use of seven colors in this piece to Trip around the World quilt (fig. 148). Descended in the Phares and Anna Hershey Snyder family, who lived in the Lititz area. Maker unknown, Warwick Township, c. 1900. Pieced cotton top, cotton batting, cotton back, 82" square. *Private collection.*

Left:
Fig. 199
Rainbow quilt, one of several belonging to the Myers, a Church of the Brethren family living near New Holland in eastern Lancaster County. Quilting was done in waffle pattern throughout the central portion, with a cable pattern in the border. Made for Amanda Myer (1859-1938) before her marriage to Henry Metzler. Attributed to Amanda and her mother Leah Reif Myer (1833-1918), Earl Township, c. 1880. Pieced cotton top, cotton batting, cotton back, 85" x 79". *Collection of Dorothy Jean Hess.*

Below:
Fig. 200
Rainbow crib quilt said to be put together from scraps of Rainbow quilts (fig. 199) made by Amanda Myer Metzler, owner of several Rainbow quilts. Random piecing and haphazard semi-circular quilting patterns lend charm to this child's bedcover. Amanda Myer Metzler (1859-1938), Earl Township, early 1900s. *Collection of Arlene H. Hess.*

Chapter Seventeen

QUILTS AND MORE

The Pennsylvania Germans seemed to delight in living with colorful decoration. Paint-decorated dower chests; brilliantly grained cupboards, bucket benches, and hanging shelves; brightly penned fraktur; and handwoven coverlets of the brightest hues are a few examples of common household objects uncommonly and delightfully decorated. So it is not hard to understand how the traditional quiltmaking skills might have been applied to less common fabric forms for added decorative effects.

Decorated pillowcases with or without matching quilts are commonly found in areas of Pennsylvania settled by the Germans. Occasionally they were embellished with block prints, more often needlework, and most commonly with appliqued or pieced work. A pair of pillowcases and an accompanying quilt (figs. 201 and 202) have been attributed to Sarah Graybill Diller. Although not much is known about the maker, an undated typed note on the pillowcases from the present owner's grandmother reads: "These pillow cases were made/ over 100 years ago./Mrs. Annie E. Baker."

The type of fabrics used and the large size of the quilt suggest that these textiles were made in the early 1800s. Two related quilts, featuring large central stars and attributed to the same maker, also survive. In place of a white background, one of them contains figured glazed chintz material. The quilts and pillowcases were pieced by hand and share similar small-print cottons and a white cotton background. Like the majority of pieced and appliqued pillowcases, these are not quilted, but they are edged with a hand-crocheted

Fig. 201
Pair of Sunburst pillowcases, among earliest of this form documented; they appear to have been made to use with a Sunburst quilt (fig. 202). Typed note attached to pillowcases reads, "These pillow cases were made/over 100 years ago./Mrs. Annie E. Baker." (Note written before 1936, the year Mrs. Baker died.) All pieces attributed to Sarah Graybill Diller (dates unknown), Lancaster County, early 1800s. Pieced cotton tops, no quilting, cotton backs, cotton crocheted lace edging, 28" x 19". *Collection of John M. Whittock, Jr.*

Fig. 202
Sunburst quilt that matches pillowcases (fig. 201); well-executed pinwheel and waffle quilting fills open areas and undulating feather design adds to border interest. Attributed to the maker of the pillowcases, Sarah Graybill Diller (dates unknown), Lancaster County, early 1800s. 1830. Pieced cotton top, cotton batting, cotton back, 98" square. *Collection of John M. Whittock, Jr.*

Above:
Fig. 203
Pair of Floral appliqued pillowcases, made to complement Floral appliqued quilt (fig. 204). Marked with appliqued letters "MG," attributed to Mary Grumbine (dates unknown), Earl Township, late 1800s. Appliqued cotton top, no quilting, cotton back, ruffled cotton edging, 31" x 17.75". *Private collection.*

Right:
Fig. 204
Floral appliqued quilt accompanying previous pillowcases. Pattern is more intricate, with a different selection of appliqued fabric but sharing the same appliqued initials, "MG," and yellow ground material as the pillowcases. Attributed to Mary Grumbine (dates unknown), Earl Township, late 1800s. Appliqued cotton top, cotton batting, cotton back, 92" square. *Private collection.*

lace. The quilt, however, is densely quilted throughout, the pattern conforming to the piecing. Diamond, feather, and cable patterns fill the open white areas. Although sets of bedcoverings were likely quite common, these are the earliest survivals found during the Quilt Harvest project.

A later quilt and pillowcase set (figs. 203 and 204) is attributed by the family to Mary Grumbine of New Holland. All pieces bear her initials "MG." Although little is known about the maker, she probably created them in the 1870s. Mary's pillowcases were not quilted, either, and have a red ruffle on the opening edges. Bright yellow as well as bright orange backgrounds are found most frequently in quilts made in the northern part of Lancaster County and adjacent Lebanon and Berks Counties. That choice of color and the vigorous vine, floral, and leaf applique create a lively set of bedcoverings.

It is unknown whether a set of pillowcases that belonged in the Geib family of Manheim (fig. 205) ever had a matching quilt. The pillowcases appear to have been made in the 1830s or 1840s and are unusual because both sides have distinct designs and are fully quilted. The quilting patterns follow the pieced design and employ heart-shaped scrolls and flowering plants in the open white areas.

An interesting group of Irish Chain patterned materials was produced in the early 1900s by two maiden sisters, Ann and Rachel Shenk. At the estate sale of their niece in Elizabethtown, where they lived all of their lives, there was a complete set of bedcoverings: quilt, bolster cover, and pillowcases. Also

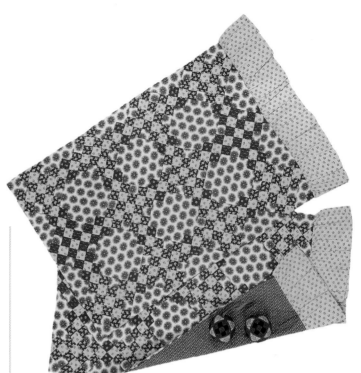

Fig. 206
Pair of Irish Chain pillow cases and fabric balls made by two maiden sisters known to neighbors as Aunties Ann and Rachel Shenk (dates unknown), West Donegal Township, early 1900s. Pillow cases: pieced cotton front, cotton back, ruffled cotton edge, 27" x 16.5"; fabric balls: pieced cotton and silk velvet, feather stitch decoration, 2.5" diameter. *Private collection.*

sold were at least six sets of pillowcases in the Irish Chain pattern and a pair of pieced fabric balls made from the same materials used in many of the pillowcases (fig. 206). One wonders if these maiden ladies, known by their neighbors as Auntie Ann and Auntie Rachel, were addicted to the Irish Chain pattern. All of their work was done with brightly printed cotton fabrics, and each pillowcase was trimmed with a wide solid-colored ruffle.

Pieced fabric balls like those made by the Shenk sisters are unusual. They seem to be found most frequently in the Elizabethtown, Mount Joy, and Manheim areas of the County. The two illustrated here are quite firm, and they rattle if shaken. Some are softer and do not have a hollow center. Others are actually made from pieces resembling orange sections, tied at their ends, and fitted snugly together. A variety of these decorative balls are pictured here (fig. 207). Each has hanging loops made of folded fabric or string. Some have a history of being given as tokens of friendship, and they usually appear in good condition with no evidence of having been used as toys or pin cushions.[41]

Another less common form of quiltmaking is the hanging bag (fig. 208). This example has two hanging loops at the top edges and a slit along the right side for an opening. The back is made from a printed fabric and the edges are secured with a cloth binding, much as a quilt might be. They were hung on the walls of Pennsylvania German homes to use as convenient containers for fabric scraps and other sundries. Some even held necessary paper on the

Fig. 205
Pair of Star pillowcases, unusual because they have patterns on both sides and are quilted over both surfaces with vigorous heart-shaped scrolls and flowerpot designs. Made by a member of the Geib family, Rapho Township, c. 1835. Pieced cotton and quilted both sides, 27" x 17.5". *Private collection.*

Fig. 207
Grouping of pieced solid and segmented fabric balls with hanging loops. Such objects frequently were given as presents or tokens of friendship. These have no evidence of being used as pincushions or toys. Segmented balls *(center and lower right)* unfold into a series of segments resembling peeled orange sections joined at their ends. The pair of solid wool balls with feather stitch decoration *(lower left)* were owned by the Aaron Hoover family, Mennonites living in Brownstown, West Earl Township. The small ball *(top center)* is made from velvets and silks and decoration resembling a crazy quilt. Two balls *(top right)* with orange fabric strips, similar to balls in the previous illustration, (fig. 206), both rattle when shaken and were found in the Elizabethtown area of West Donegal Township. Assorted fabrics, wool, cotton, silk, silk velvet, feather stitch decoration, sizes vary from 2.5" to 3.5" diameter. *Private collection.*

Fig. 208
Log Cabin hanging bag, often used to hold fabrics and sewing materials in the home and sometimes paper in the outhouse. Exquisitely pieced printed cottons surrounding central square with cross-stitched initials "AB," attributed to Church of the Brethren member Anna Bowman, who later married Ferris B. Rudy. Anna Bowman (1853-1929), Warwick Township, c. 1870. Pieced and folded cotton with cross stitching, no quilting, cotton back and hanging loops, right side opening. 18" square. *Collection of Jim and Nan Tshudy.*

Fig. 209
Center Square hanging bag, carefully pieced, using English glazed chintz fabric manufactured in the 1840s, bordered with a contrasting seam containing flat piping insert; the central white square is closely quilted to add to the decorative effect. The attached tag reading "Katie W. Brubaker/ Dec. 25, 1879" would suggest that it was a Christmas present to young Katie (1868-1897) from her mother Anna Bair Wissler (Mrs. Benjamin) Brubaker (1846-1936), Manor Township, mid 1800s. Pieced cotton top with quilting, cotton back, cotton, right side opening, 25" square. *Private collection.*

outhouse wall. This finely executed Log Cabin design is cross stitched in the center square with the intitials "AB." It is attributed to Anna Bowman, the daughter of John and Susan Lausch Bowman. A member of the Church of the Brethren, she lived on a farm near the village of Kissel Hill in Warwick Township. It would have been made sometime before her marriage to Ferris B. Rudy in the early 1870s.

Only occasionally were hanging bags quilted (fig. 209). The central white diamond of this unusual piece is heavily quilted with a variety of parallel, zig-zag, and diamond quilting patterns. The paper tag sewn on the front surface reads "Katie W. Brubaker/Dec. 25, 1879." A narrow strip of brown printed material was inserted as piping into the seam that borders the large-print chintz. The highly glazed chintz material in the outer triangles was carefully chosen and was cut to form a balanced frame for the central quilted area. The fabric, containing flowers in reserves on a dotted ground, is an English roller print manufactured sometime between 1835 and 1840.[42] The remaining

materials used in the piece appear to date from the same period. Special thought and attention to detail were given to the construction of this bag.

Likely the bag was a treasured family piece handed down as a Christmas gift to Katie in 1879.

She was the daughter of Annie B. Wissler and Benjamin Brubaker, a Mennonite couple living in Manor Township in southwestern Lancaster County. Katie, who was eleven years old when she received the piece, later married Elias L. Herr. This piece and another hanging bag, dated 1864 with Katie's mother's name on it, were passed down and treasured by the Herr family until sold at public auction in 1984.

Appliqued hanging bags are less common than pieced examples. The one pictured (fig. 210) is of a rather large size, having three loops across the top and a side opening. The opening, on the left side of the bag, is secured with two blue-decorated white porcelain buttons. Openings are usually found on the right side of a hanging bag, but occasionally they were accessed from

Fig. 210
Floral appliqued hanging bag, large enough to have three hanging loops with opening on left side. Most open on the right, and occasionally some open on the top. Was this maker left-handed? Cross stitching reads, "Martha B. Geist, June1,/M B/in the year/ 1851." Maker was probably Martha Burkholder Geist, West Lampeter Township, 1851. Appliqued cotton and cross stitching, no quilting, cotton back, cotton twill tapes, porcelain buttons, 25" square. *Private collection.*

Fig. 211
Single pocket with matching needle case, decorated with silk ribbon and rosettes, a common embellishment on samplers made in the first half of the 1800s in southeastern Pennsylvania. Women's pieced pockets were in common use by women of English extraction but were rarely found in Pennsylvania German households. Maker unknown, Lancaster County, c. 1840. Pocket: pieced cotton front, silk rosettes, cotton tape binding and tie, 9.75" x 8.5"; needle case: cardboard covered with cotton and wool, silk rosettes, cotton tape binding, wool sheaves, and cotton twine closure, 3.75" x 3" closed. *Private collection.*

Fig. 212
Floral appliqued hand towel, showing an unusual form of decoration on a common Pennsylvania German household object. Commonly decorated with cross stitching and hung as decoration on doors, the towel is a rare survivor. Maker unknown, southeastern Pennsylvania, c. 1840. Appliqued cotton, applied cotton ruffles to top and bottom, cotton twill tape loops, 59" x 15.5". *Private collection.*

Fig. 213
Center Diamond seat cushion laid out in design similar to Amish quilt top. Brightly colored, decorative, and functional articles similar to this are commonly seen in Amish homes. Unknown Amish maker, Lancaster County, c. 1945. Pieced wool top with cotton feather stitching, unknown stuffing, wool knit sides, wool hen's nest stitched back, rayon cording, 17" x 17" x 6". *Heritage Center of Lancaster County through the generosity of an anonymous donor.*

the top. This bag is bound with a white commercially woven cotton binding often seen on white background quilts of the same mid-1800s era. Fortunately, the owner of this piece documented it well by cross stitching "Martha B. Geist, June 1,/MB/in the year/1851" on the top surface. The maker and owner was probably Martha Burkholder Geist, the daughter of John and Susanna Burkholder Geist. She grew up in East Lampeter Township, where her father was a wagon maker and farmer. Martha later married the Rev. Abraham Kurtz.[43]

Women's pieced pockets, in pairs and by themselves, are found in households in traditionally English families living in the Delaware Valley, but they appear less commonly in Lancaster County. Occasionally woven linen pockets, either plain or decorated with Pennsylvania German cross stitching, are discovered, but pieced Pennsylvania German pockets (fig. 211) are a rarity. The example illustrated has tape ties to place around the waist and a front slit for access to the pocket. Added to the pieced block decoration on the front surface are silk rosettes that adorn the corners and edges of the opening. They are similar to rosettes used on the corners of early 1800s samplers found in southeastern Pennsylvania. The piece appears to have been made between 1835 and 1840. Inside the pocket the matching needlecase with similar rosettes was found.

Another decorative object, frequently hung in Pennsylvania German homes, was the decorated hand towel. Most commonly such pieces were decorated with colored cross stitching and drawn work designs.[44] Rarely was a hand towel decorated by appliqueing fabric (fig. 212). Little is known about this piece, but the fabrics appear to be from the 1840s. Two tape loops were applied for hanging, and the bottom edge is finished with a ruffle.

The Amish enjoy bright and colorful objects in their homes. For the most part they are functional items such as a seat cushion (fig. 213). Reminiscent of the Center Diamond pattern used on their quilts, this cushion is made of heavier, more serviceable wools than a quilt would be. The colors chosen reflect the typical Amish color preference away from the pure primary color spectrum.

The hot pads or potholders (fig. 214) are another example of small useful items made more colorful than necessary by the use of scraps of clothing material. The four potholders with notes pinned in the center were made from scraps as a gift for Paul Young in 1922, when he was one year old, by his Grandma Sherich. The family lived in the Landisville area at the time. The red pad was found in an Amish home and probably dates from the 1920s, too. It also appears to have been made from clothing scraps, and it was decorated and bound with velvet and silk grosgrain ribbon. Little is known about the

other pads pictured, but they illustrate how carefully pieced even such incidental objects can be.

One of the most interesting, extensive, and varied collections of three-dimensional objects that has come to light is the work of Reba Groff (fig. 215). Little is known about the maker other than the information she wrote on tags sewn on the bottoms of some of her cloth figures. It is thought that she was a Mennonite or Church of the Brethren woman who ran a small gift shop from her home in the rural New Holland area. She wrote "Reba Groff/New Holland/R.D.1" on the bottom of a grouping of hen and chicks. On the two eagles she penned, "God Bless/You All/Christmas 1940" and "To Lizzy/From Reba." At least twenty-two of her sculptures are known to exist. It is not necessary to know more specific information of the maker to enjoy these charming little pieces and know that the recipients received a great deal of pleasure from them, too.

Indeed all of the objects in this chapter, many of which were functional household items, continue to provide colorful decoration to our lives and homes. They give us pleasure and speak to us of a time and people far removed from our daily routine. Knowing more about the objects and why they were made helps us better understand the people who made them.

Fig. 214
Grouping of pieced hot pads, decorative but useful items found in many Pennsylvania German homes, frequently given as gifts to friends and relatives. The round red wool pad *(upper left)* with applied wool embroidery, silk ribbon binding, and applied velvet tape, and cotton batting is Amish. The grouping of four round potholders *(bottom center)* was made by Grandmother Sherich (dates unknown), East Hempfield Township, for grandson Paul Young in 1922. His name is on each label. She was a young widow and a member of Church of the Brethren who made them for each of her grandsons. Other potholders are by unknown makers, Lancaster County, all made in the early 1900s. Assorted pieced cotton fabric tops and binding, woven material filling, and cotton batting, cotton and wool backs, sizes vary from 5" to 7" diameter. *Collections of Alice Jane Herr Young Walter; the Heritage Center of Lancaster County, through the generosity of Drs. Irwin M. and Susan Richman; and private collections.*

Fig. 215
Part of a collection of twenty-two fabric sculptures made by Reba Groff, a Plain Sect woman who was thought to have run a gift shop in her home near New Holland. Many pieces bear sewn-on fabric labels penned with "Reba Groff." Hen and chicks have label reading "Reba Groff/New Holland/R.D.1." One baldheaded eagle label reads "To Lizzie/From Reba." Large maroon eagle label notes "God Bless/You All/Christmas 1940." Collection includes figures representing Jonah and the whale, busts of Presidents Lincoln and Washington, a family of mice, a variety of birds, and a turtle. Reba Groff (dates unknown), Earl Township, c. 1940. Cardboard and unspun cotton covered with pieced wool and cotton; applied cotton, wool and silk ribbon and embroidery; sizes vary up to 8" maximum dimension. *Collection of Ron and Marilyn Kowaleski.*

CONCLUSION

It's a sunny day in early June of the year 1914. The morning dew glistens and the scent of fresh-mown grass and newly cultivated soil from the kitchen garden hangs in the air at Christ Snyder's home place, Willow Spring Farm, in Clay Township, Lancaster County. The daughters and granddaughters of Simon B. and Fanny S. Bucher Snyder, along with their youngest children, have gathered for quilting and rag carpet sewing. They have set up their quilting frame, benches, and sewing machine under the trees on the east side of the house (fig. 216). The group, who call themselves "the girl cousins," often meet with a few neighbors for this sort of activity. Christian Snyder and his six sisters, most of whom are pictured here, were born in the house.

The tobacco and wood sheds provide a background for the group as they interrupt their morning activities to pose for neighbor Hannah Kreiter Wissler, who has a keen interest in photography. She quickly takes her place in the foreground on the right side of the picture, holding the string that will release the shutter. Absent from the photograph are Lizzie and Lavina Snyder. Christ's wife Sadie died five years earlier and he has not yet remarried, so his younger maiden sisters, Lizzie and Lavina, are inside preparing dinner for the day of quilting.

Dinner on the farm is a noon meal. Here at the table (fig. 217), Hannah Wissler captures that moment before heads are bowed in prayer.[45] The picnic tables and benches are put together to seat the large gathering. Homespun linen tablecloths cover the tables, which are decorated with vases of flowers picked from plantings near the house. The meal will take place on the shady, cooler north side of the limestone family home built by Georg Illig in 1781. Lizzie and Lavina appear in this photograph, ready to serve their guests after a busy morning of quilting and socializing.

Quilting in such groups was common practice for Lancaster County women. The majority (90 percent) of Lancaster quilters for whom there was background information in the Quilt Harvest study had at some time quilted in a group. The activity might have been with mostly family members, as seen here, or with friends or church members.

Seated at the base of the tree, wearing a dark dress, is Barbara Bucher Snyder Stoner, the maker of an intricately pieced Sampler quilt (fig. 218). She made the quilt for herself right here at Willow Spring farm before her marriage to John M. Stoner in 1884. Next to her, at the sewing machine, is her daughter Ida Stoner Horst, for whom Barbara made a Philadelphia Pavement quilt (fig. 61). Also seated among the women at the back of the quilting frame is Amanda Snyder Landis, the maker of a Papercut crib quilt (fig. 127). Her daughter, Vera Snyder Landis, for whom that small quilt was made, sits at the feet of Barbara Bucher Snyder Stoner.

Fig. 216
Photograph taken by Hannah Kreiter Wissler (1884-1978), Clay Township, amateur photographer, pictured on far right holding string that will trip the shutter to make an image. Pictured here are daughters and granddaughters of Simon R. and Fanny S. Bucher and some of their friends and neighbors. Ink inscription identifies scene as "Quilting and sewing carpet rags at brother Christs/home, June. 2. 1914." "Brother Christs home" refers to Willow Spring Farm, the Clay Township residence of Christian B. Snyder and family. *Image courtesy of Willow Spring Farm.*

An icon of Lancaster County pieced work, Barbara's Sampler quilt is one of a small group of closely related bedcoverings produced in northeastern Lancaster County. Barbara is said to have worked on her quilt for several years, usually in the evening after her household chores were finished. According to relatives, she copied patterns from oilcloth flooring she had seen in homes and interior architectural details in churches her family visited. She was chided about not hearing the sermons because she was busy sketching her quilt patterns. One of the most elaborate blocks in the quilt is made up of 144 separate pieces.

However, she may have received her inspiration and certainly received her instruction from her mother, Fanny Bucher Snyder, who was probably the maker of an earlier related Sampler quilt (fig. 219). Similar in design, but based on diamond-shaped blocks instead of squares, the quilt has Fanny's maiden name initials "FSB" outlined in embroidery on the back. The letters "HW," probably for the intended recipient, along with the date 1860, appear inked on the front surface. At one time the quilt also had a fringe.

The family always considered Barbara's quilt her best one, and it was "sort of a practice" not to use some of the better quilts. Other quilts made by women in the photographs were kept "just for nice" by family members.[46] When visitors came on Sundays after church, and perhaps even on this second day of June 1914, the quilts were brought out and shown. This ritual is a well-known practice among the Pennsylvania German women in Lancaster County and would have been an opportunity to share quilting patterns and expertise among family members and friends.

These engaging and informative images represent family and commu-

nity involvement in quiltmaking. Even the young children are occupied with some sewing-related activity. Scraps of material, not to be wasted, are being cut and sewn together in long strips to be taken later to a professional weaver, where they will be woven into rag carpet. Friends and relatives come together to create quilts, share companionship, break bread, and honor their Maker. Hannah Wissler's photographs not only chronicle the Snyder family activities but also help us appreciate these pieces from the past, so we are better able to understand the quilting traditions of Lancaster County.

Fig. 217
Photograph taken by Hannah Wissler of noon dinner table at the moment before saying grace. Pictured here are the "girl cousins," as they called themselves when they gathered for such events, along with some neighbor women, just before giving grace after a morning of quilting. Ink inscription notes, "This is where we had our dinner/the day of the quilting. June. 2. 1914." *Image courtesy of Willow Spring Farm.*

Fig. 218
Sampler quilt, made of many small pieces—one square is pieced from 144 bits of material—by Barbara Bucher Snyder. Made before her marriage to John Musselman Stoner in the house pictured in the photograph of the quilting party dinner table (fig. 217). Barbara Bucher Snyder (1862-1922), Clay Township, c. 1880. Pieced cotton top, cotton batting, cotton back, 90" x 82.5". *Private collection.* Photograph by Charles Studio of Photography.

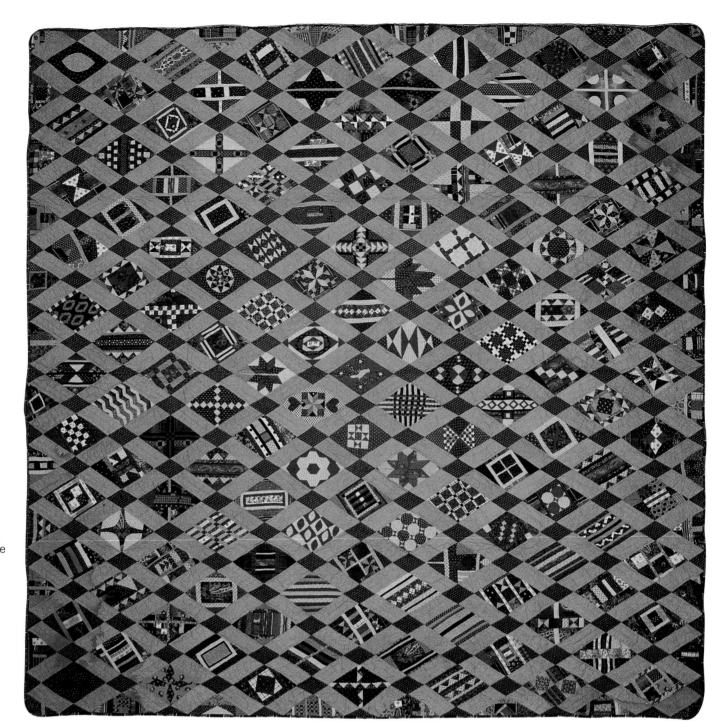

Fig. 219
Sampler quilt, similar to Barbara Bucher Snyder's quilt (fig. 218), but worked in diamond blocks instead of squares. The initials "FSB" are embroidered on the back and initials and date "HW/1860," for the intended recipient, are printed in ink on a small white block in the center of the quilt. Attributed to Barbara's mother Fanny S. Bucher (1841-1910), Warwick Township, 1860. Pieced cotton top with ink lettering, cotton batting, cotton back embroidered initials, 84" square.
Collection of Clark E. Hess.

FOOTNOTES

[1]"Garden Spot" is a term first used in the early 1800s by observers of the area's attractive green landscape. In this century the term has also been used to promote the area on behalf of its highly productive agricultural acreage. Gerald S. Lestz, personal communication, October 20, 1999.

[2]Barbara Brackman, *Encyclopedia of Pieced Quilt Patterns* (Paducah, Kentucky: American Quilter's Society, 1993), pp. 208-209.

[3]For more detailed information on template quiltmaking see Virginia Gunn, "Template Quilt Construction and Its Offshoots." *Pieced By Mother: Symposium Papers*, edited by Jeannette Lasansky (Lewisburg, Pennsylvania: Oral Traditions Project, 1988), pp 69-75.

[4]Brackman, *Encyclopedia of Pieced Quilt Patterns*, p.525.

[5]More information on the Lititz Moravian Girls' School can be found in Patricia T. Herr, "The Ornamental Branches": *Needlework and Arts from the Lititz Moravian Girls' School* (Virginia Beach: The Donning Company, 1996).

[6]Information taken from *Store Book 1805-1806* Box IX A Linden Hall Archives, Lititz, Pa.

[7]*Biographical Annals of Lancaster County Pennsylvania*, (Philadelphia, Pennsylvania: J. H. Beers & Co., 1903), p. 1447.

[8]Lloyd Huber Bomberger, *Bomberger Lancaster County Roots 1722-1986* (Lancaster, Pennsylvania: Stauffer Printing Service, 1986), pp. 58-63 and 113.

[9]For further information on the Pennsylvania German dowry see Jeannette Lansansky, *A Good Start: The Aussteier or Dowry* (Lewisburg, Pennsylvania: The Oral Traditions Project, 1990).

[10]Theodore W. Herr, *Genealogical Record of Reverend Hans Herr and His Direct Lineal Descendants* (1908; reprint, Lancaster, Pennsylvania: Lancaster Mennonite Historical Society, 1980), pp. 29 and 107.

[11]This phrase was used first by Quaker John Reynall in 1738, in a letter to David Flennegin in London ordering furniture including, "2 raised Japan'd Black Corner Cubbards, with 2 Doors to each, no Red in 'em of the best Sort, but Plain." Quoted in Frederick B. Tolles, *Meeting House and Counting House: The Quaker Merchants of Colonial Philadelphia 1682-1763* (New York: W.W. Norton & Company, Inc., 1963), p.128.

[12]More detailed information on early Quaker settlement and quilting in Pennsylvania may be found in Patricia T. Herr, "All in Modesty and Plainness," *The Quilt Digest* 3, edited by Michael M. Kile (San Francisco: The Quilt Digest Press, 1985), pp. 22-35, and other more recent sources exploring Quaker quilts listed in the bibliography.

[13]Charles D. Spotts, "The Pilgrim's Pathway: The Underground Railroad in Lancaster County," *Community Historians Annual*, No. 5, December 1966 (Lancaster, Pennsylvania: Franklin and Marshall College Library), pp. 30-32 and 38.

[14]Marianne Gibbons diaries, 1892, 1893.

[15]Marianne Gibbons diary, 1894.

[16]See Dr. Donald B.Kraybill, "The Amish of Lancaster County," introduction to *Amish Arts of Lancaster County*, by Patricia T. Herr (Atlgen, Pennsylvania: Schiffer Publications Ltd., 1998).

[17]Consult the bibliography for a variety of publications pertaining to the Lancaster Amish community, quilts, and decorative arts of the Amish.

[18]More information on fabric sources of Amish quilters may be found in Eve Wheatcroft Granick, *The Amish Quilt* (Intercourse, Pennsylvania: Good Books, 1989), pp. 57-71.

[19]Interviews with Bill Greenberg and Joyce Brown of Greenberg Company, Intercourse, Pennsylvania, August 8, 1992, by Patricia Keller and the author on the occasion of Bill Greenberg's eightieth birthday party and at his home in Philadelphia, September 3, 1992, by Pat Keller, Quilt Harvest Data, collection of the Heritage Center of Lancaster County.

[20]Rebecca Lapp, diary, November 11, 1886. Private collection. Rebecca (1873-1905) was the youngest daughter of Rebecca Lantz Lapp and Michael K. Lapp. Her older brother was Henry Lapp, well-known Amish furniture maker and folk artist. They lived in an area known as Groff's Store near the present village of Mascot in Leacock Township.

[21]See Clayton H. Gehman, *Children of the Conestoga* (Elgin, Illinois: Brethren Press, 1978), p. 18.

[22]*Ibid.*, p.15.

[23]The author is indebted to family quilt researcher Mary Jo Scott for sharing her carefully compiled and extensive research for this book.

[24]Interview with Mabel Bryant Joseph, Smyrna, Delaware, October 29, 1999, by Kim Fortney and Patricia T. Herr, Quilt Harvest Data, collection of the Heritage Center of Lancaster County.

[25]The whereabouts of the other, made for grandson Jacob Carpenter Hess, is unknown.

[26]Elizabeth (Lizzie) Rupp Burkholder (Mrs. Wayne) Carpenter (1857-1944), Harriet Carpenter's daughter-in-law, would regularly bring out the family quilts made by Harriet to show Sunday afternoon visitors. Great-granddaughter Mabel Bryant (born 1905) was present during her childhood at many of the gatherings and fondly remembers hearing about her great-grandmother's quiltmaking. One of the women, who according to Lizzie, quilted with Harriet was a Mrs. Habecker. One cannot assume this was Susan Frey Shenk Habecker, as she lived more than twelve miles away in East Hempfield Township. Information recorded during interview with Mabel Bryant Joseph, October 29, 1999.

[27]Both quilts are located at the International Quilt Study Center, Lincoln, Nebraska.

[28]Groundbreaking work on the subject was written by Dena S. Katzenberg in *Baltimore Album Quilts* (Baltimore: Baltimore Museum of Art, 1981). Further work in an ongoing series of books is being written by Elly Sienkiewicz, *Baltimore Beauties and Beyond*, (Martinez, California: C & T Publishing, 1991).

[29]Katzenberg, *Baltimore Album Quilts*, p.46.

[30]For further information on constructing Papercut applique see Elly Sienkiewicz, *Baltimore Beauties and Beyond, Studies in Classic Album Quilt Applique, Volume III*, Part 2, "Papercuts and Plenty: Papercuts in Applique, Papercuts in Albums," (Martinez, California: C & T Publishing, 1995), pp. 37-54.

[31]*Biographical Annals of Lancaster County Pennsylvania*, (Philadelphia, Pennsylvania: J. H. Beers & Co., 1903), pp. 264-66, 324-25, and 662.

[32]*Ibid.*, pp. 473-74 and 774-75.

[33]Fabric composition and quilting patterns of Hawaiian quilts is markedly different than that found in Pennsylvania German quilts of Lancaster County. For comparison on this point see the extensive catalogue of Hawaiian quilts written by Reiko Mochinaga Brandon, *The Hawaiian Quilt* (Tokyo: Kokusia Art, 1989).

[34]Genealogical information may be found in Beiler, Katie, ed. *Descendants and History of Christian Fisher (1757-1838)* (Soudersburg, Pennsylvania: Eby's Quality Printing, 1988), Lydia Fisher Petersheim # 6460 and Lydia F. Kauffman #2687.

[35]McCauley, Daniel and Kathryn, *Decorative Arts of the Amish of Lancaster County* (Intercourse, Pennsylvania: Good Books), pp. 62-63.

[36]The database information from the Quilt Harvest project reveals that only 16 percent of the quilts seen have some form of appliqued work on them, 78 percent of the quilts seen were pieced work, and about 6 percent were whole cloth quilts.

[37]Landis, Ira D., *The Landis Family Book Section II* (Bareville, Pennsylvania: Ira D. Landis, 1952), pp. 304-11.

[38]Beiler, Katie, ed. *Descendants and History of Christian Fisher* (Soudersburg, Pennsylvania: Eby's Quality Printing, 1988), pp. 103 and 175.

[39]Lasansky, Jeannette, *Pieced by Mother: Over 100 Years of Quiltmaking Traditions* (Lewisburg, Pennsylvania: Oral Traditions Project, 1987), pp. 26-28,42-45, 92, 102, and 103.

[40]Petrone, Gerard S., MD, *Tobacco Advertising the Great Seduction* (Atlglen, Pennsylvania: Schiffer Publishing Ltd., 1996), p. 167. Burdick, J. R., *The American Card Catalogue* (Syracuse: J. R. Burdick, 1953), pp. 42-47.

[41] More information on three-dimensional Pennsylvania German fabric forms may be found in Patricia T.Herr, "Iwwerich Un Ender: "Those Small Pieced, Appliqued, and Quilted Objects in the Pennsylvania-German Household," *Bits and Pieces*, Jeanette Lasansky, ed. (Lewisburg, Pennsylvania: Oral Traditions Project, 1991) pp. 26-47.

[42] Florence M. Montgomery, *Printed Textiles* (New York: The Viking Press, 1970) p. 315.

[43] *Biographical Annals of Lancaster County Pennsylvania* (Philadelphia, Pennsylvania: J. H. Beers & Co., 1903), p. 487.

[44] An excellent source of information on decorated hand towels is Ellen J. Gehret, *This Is the Way I Pass My Time* (Birdsboro, Pennsylvania: The Pennsylvania German Society, 1985).

[45] The photographs illustrated here are from a group of three, taken by Hannah Wissler, that have survived in a charred photo album. The album was rescued from an attic fire that destroyed the roof of the Ilig/Snyder home at Willow Spring Farm in 1961.

[46] Extensive research on the family, their quilts, and related quilts of the Cocalico Valley is being conducted by Patricia J. Keller in connection with her doctoral thesis, working title "Quilts from Home," for the Winterthur Musuem/University of Delaware program in the History of American Civilization.

BIBLIOGRAPHY

Allen, Gloria Seaman, and Nancy Gibson Tuckhorn. *A Maryland Album: Quiltmaking Traditions, 1634-1934*. Nashville, Tennessee: Rutledge Hill Press, 1995.

The American Card Catalogue. Syracuse, New York: J. R. Burdick, 1953.

Beiler, Katie, ed. *Descendants and History of Christian Fisher (1757-1838)*. Soudersburg, Pennsylvania: Eby's Quality Printing, 1988.

Biographical Annals of Lancaster County. Philadelphia: J. H. Beers & Co., 1903.

Bomberger, Lloyd H. *Bomberger Lancaster County Roots, 1722-1986*. Lancaster, Pennsylvania.: Stauffer Printing Service, 1986.

Brackman, Barbara. *Encyclopedia of Applique: An Illustrated, Numerical Index to Traditional and Modern Patterns*. McLean, Virginia: EPM Publications, Inc., 1993.

___, comp. *Encyclopedia of Pieced Quilt Patterns*. Paducah, Kentucky: American Quilter's Society, 1993.

Brandon, Reiko Mochinaga. *The Hawaiian Quilt*. Tokyo: Kokusia Art, 1989.

Community Historians Annual, No. 5. Lancaster, Pennsylvania: Franklin and Marshall College Library, 1966.

Erb, Emma. Diary, 1917. Penn Township, Lancaster County, Pennsylvania. Collection of Anna Mary Miller and Diane Fisher.

Garvan, Beatrice B., and Charles F. Hummel. *The Pennsylvania Germans: A Celebration of Their Arts, 1683-1850*. Philadelphia: Philadelphia Museum of Art, 1982.

Gehman, Clayton H. *Children of the Conestoga*. Elgin, Illinois: Brethren Press, 1978.

Gehret, Ellen J. *This Is the Way I Pass My Time*. Vol. XVIII. Birdboro, Pennsylvania: The Pennsylvania German Society, 1985.

Gibbons, Marianne. Diaries, 1892-94. Bird-In-Hand, Upper Leacock Township, Lancaster County, Pennsylvania. Collection of John H. Brubaker III.

Gingerich, Hugh F., and Rachel W. Kreider. *Amish and Amish Mennonite Genealogies*. Gordonville, Pennsylvania: Pequea Publishers, 1986.

Granick, Eve Wheatcroft. *The Amish Quilt*. Intercourse, Pennsylvania: Good Books, 1989.

Herr, Patricia T. *Amish Arts of Lancaster County*. Atglen, Pennsylvania: Schiffer Publishing Ltd., 1998.

___. *"The Ornamental Branches": Needlework and Arts from the Lititz Moravian Girls' School*. Virginia Beach, Virginia: The Donning Company, 1996.

Herr, Theodore W. *Genealogical Record of Reverend Hans Herr and His Direct Lineal Descendants*. 1908. Reprint, Lancaster, Pennsylvania: Lancaster Mennonite Historical Society, 1980.

Holstein, Jonathan. *The Pieced Quilt: An American Tradition*. Greenwich, Connecticut: New York Graphic Society Ltd., 1973.

Katzenberg, Dena S. *Baltimore Album Quilts*. Baltimore: The Baltimore Museum of Art, 1981.

Keller, Patricia J. *"Of the Best Sort but Plain": Quaker Quilts From the Delaware Valley, 1760-1890*. Chadds Ford, Pennsylvania: Brandywine River Museum, 1996.

Kile, Michael M., ed. *The Quilt Digest*. San Francisco: The Quilt Digest Press, 1985.

Kraybill, Donald B., Patricia T. Herr, and Jonathan Holstein. *A Quiet Spirit: Amish Quilts from the Collection of Cindy Tietze and Stuart Hodosh*. Los Angeles: UCLA Fowler Museum of Cultural History, 1996.

Landis, Ira D. *The Landis Family Book, Section II*. Bareville, Pennsylvania: Ira D. Landis, 1952.

Lapp, Rebecca. Diary, November 11, 1886. Groff's Store, Leacock Township, Lancaster County, Pennsylvania. Private collection.

Lasansky, Jeannette, ed. *Bits and Pieces: Textile Traditions*. Lewisburg, Pennsylvania: Oral Traditions Project of the Union County Historical Society, 1991.

___. *A Good Start: The Aussteier or Dowry*. Lewisburg, Pennsylvania: Oral Traditions Project of the Union County Historical Society, 1990.

___, ed. *In the Heart of Pennsylvania: Symposium Papers*. Lewisburg, Pennsylvania: Oral Traditions Project of the Union County Historical Society, 1986.

___. *Pieced by Mother: Over 100 Years of Quiltmaking Traditions*. Lewisburg, Pennsylvania: Oral Traditions Project of the Union County Historical Society, 1987.

___, ed. *Pieced by Mother: Symposium Papers*. Lewisburg, Pennsylvania: Oral Traditions Project of the Union County Historical Society, 1988.

McCauley, Daniel and Kathryn. *Decorative Arts of the Amish of Lancaster County*. Intercourse, Pennsylvania: Good Books, 1988.

Miller, E. Willard, ed. *A Geography of Pennsylvania*. University Park, Pennsylvania: The Pennsylvania State University Press, 1995.

Montgomery, Florence M. *Printed Textiles: English and American Cottons and Linens 1700-1850*. New York: The Viking Press, 1970.

Nicoll, Jessica F. *Quilted for Friends: Delaware Valley Signature Quilts, 1840-1855*. Winterthur, Delaware: The Henry Frances Du Pont Winterthur Museum, 1986.

Orlofsky, Patsy and Myron. *Quilters in America*. New York: McGraw-Hill Book Company, 1974.

Petrone, Gerard S. *Tobacco Advertising: The Great Seduction*. Atglen, Pennsylvania: Schiffer Publishing Ltd., 1996.

Quilt Harvest Data, 1988-89. Heritage Center Museum of Lancaster County, Inc., Lancaster, Pennsylvania.

Siegrist, Joanne Hess. *Mennonite Women of Lancaster County: A Story in Photographs from 1855-1935*. Intercourse, Pennsylvania: Good Books, 1996.

Sienkiewicz, Elly. *Baltimore Beauties and Beyond: Studies in Classic Album Quilt Applique*. Vol. 2. Lafayette, California: C &T Publishing, 1991.

___. *Baltimore Beauties and Beyond: Studies in Classic Album Quilt Applique*. Vol. 3. Lafayette, California: C &T Publishing, 1991.

Store Book, 1805-1806. Box IX A. Linden Hall Archives, Lititz, Pennsylvania.

Tolles, Frederick B. *Meeting House and Counting House: The Quaker Merchants of Colonial Pennsylvania, 1682-1763*. New York: W. W. Norton & Company, 1963.

Weagon, Oliver F., C.E. *New Historical Atlas of Lancaster County, Pennsylvania*. Philadelphia: Everts and Stewart, 1875.